The
ANGLER'S GUIDE
········· *to* ·········
FISH

The
ANGLER'S GUIDE
to
FISH

DK PUBLISHING, INC.

www.dk.com

A DK PUBLISHING BOOK

Devised, designed, and edited for
DK Publishing by Bookbourne Limited

Editor: Ian Wood
Art Editor: Steve Leaning
Designer: Stuart John
Fish Species Illustrator: Colin Newman
US Editor: Ray Rogers

Managing Editor: Krystyna Mayer
Managing Art Editor: Derek Coombes
Production Controller: Antony Heller

Contributors: Peter Gathercole, Trevor Housby, Dennis Moss, Bruce
Vaughan, Phill Williams

First American Edition, 1994

4 6 8 10 9 7 5

First Concise Edition, 1997

Published in the United States by DK Publishing, Inc., 95 Madison Avenue

New York, New York 10016

www.dk.com

The material in this book was previously published under the title of
The DK Encyclopedia of Fishing

Library of Congress Cataloging-in-Publication Data
Angler's guide to fish. -- 1st American ed.
    p.   cm.
  Includes indexes.
  ISBN 0-7894-1438-4
  1. Fishes. 2. Fishing.
QL615.D57 1996
597--dc20   96-30990
                                      CIP

Reproduced by Colourscan, Singapore
Printed in Hong Kong by
Wing King Tong

CONTENTS

Anatomy 8

FRESHWATER FISH

Black Bass 10
Bluegill, Crappies,
  Pumpkinseed, & Sunfish 12
Barbel, Tench, & Asp 14
Bream, Nase, & Vimba 16
Carp 18
Chub, Dace, Roach, & Rudd 20
Pike, Pickerel, &
  Muskellunge 22
Bullhead 24
Freshwater Catfish 26
Bass & Murray Cod 28
Australian Perch & Grunters 30
Perch, Sauger, Walleye,
  & Zander 32
Char 34
Salmon 36
Trout 38
Whitefish & Grayling 40

SALTWATER FISH

Bonefish, Bluefish, & Tarpon 42
Eels 44
Sea Catfish & Barracuda 46
Amberjack & Jack 48

Pompano, Jackmackerel,
  & Roosterfish 50
Cobia, Snook, & Barramundi 52
Surfperch 54
Cod, Hake, Ling, & Burbot 56
Billfish & Swordfish 58
Wrasse & Dolphinfish 60
Snapper 62
Mullet 64
Flatfish 66
Rays 68
Skates 70
Drum & Kahawai 72
Mackerel 74
Tuna & Wahoo 76
Bonito & Shad 78
Sharks 80
Grouper 84
Porgy & Sea Bream 86
Sea Bream &
  Scorpion Fish 88

APPENDICES

Glossary 90
Index 93
Index of
Scientific Names 95
Acknowledgments 96

SPECIES

A SPECIES OF FISH (or any other organism) is a genetically distinct group, consisting of related individuals that resemble each other in appearance and behavior, and can breed among themselves but not – with some exceptions – with other species. Closely related species are grouped together into genera, and related genera are grouped into families.

Because the common names of fish can vary greatly from one region or country to another, biologists refer to them by their scientific names to avoid confusion. The scientific name of a species consists of two words, usually derived from Latin; the first of these defines the genus, and the second identifies the species. The brown trout, *Salmo trutta*, is thus the species *trutta* of the genus *Salmo*. It is also described as a salmonid, because it belongs to the Salmonidae family, which includes the salmon, trout, and char.

There are about 22,000 known species of fish, of which relatively few are of interest to anglers. This chapter gives brief descriptions of major sporting species, together with notes on the sort of techniques, tackle, and bait that may be used to catch them. They are grouped, as far as is practical, into freshwater and saltwater species, and arranged within these groups alphabetically by family name.

THE ANGLER'S QUARRY
The fish pursued by anglers range from small species that feed mainly on insects to voracious predators such as pike and shark.

ANATOMY

Fish can be divided broadly into two groups: those that have skeletons made of bone (the bony fish) and those with skeletons made of cartilage (the cartilaginous fish). In addition to having different skeletal materials, the two groups differ in their means of reproduction. In bony fish, with a few exceptions, the females discharge their eggs into the water, where they are fertilized by milt (semen) from the males. In cartilaginous fish, as in mammals, the eggs are fertilized within the bodies of the females. (Brief explanations of the anatomical terms used here are given in the glossary on pages 90–92.)

BONY FISH (OSTEICHTHYES)

A typical bony fish has two sets of paired fins (pectoral and pelvic) and a set of vertical fins (dorsal, anal, and tail). The four gill openings on each side of the head are covered by flattened bones, of which the operculum is the largest, and most species possess a gas-filled swim bladder. By altering the amount of gas (usually oxygen) in this bladder, a bony fish can adjust its buoyancy and maintain its chosen depth in the water without constantly swimming. Cartilaginous fish (*see opposite*) lack swim bladders and must keep swimming or sink to the bottom.

GILLS
A fish "breathes" by drawing water into its mouth, then forcing it through its gill chambers and out via the gill slits. Inside the gill chambers, delicate filaments absorb oxygen from the water and pass it into the blood, and remove carbon dioxide from the blood and then discharge it into the water.

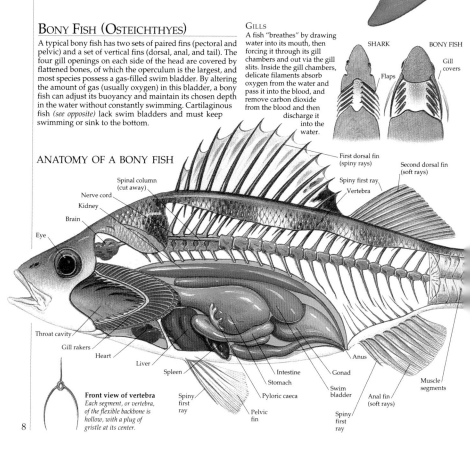

ANATOMY OF A BONY FISH

Caudal fin or tail

Skin

SHARK

BONY FISH

Flaps

Gill covers

First dorsal fin (spiny rays)

Second dorsal fin (soft rays)

Spiny first ray

Vertebra

Spinal column (cut away)

Nerve cord

Kidney

Brain

Eye

Throat cavity

Gill rakers

Heart

Liver

Spleen

Intestine

Stomach

Pyloric caeca

Gonad

Swim bladder

Anus

Muscle segments

Anal fin (soft rays)

Spiny first ray

Front view of vertebra
Each segment, or vertebra, of the flexible backbone is hollow, with a plug of gristle at its center.

Spiny first ray

Pelvic fin

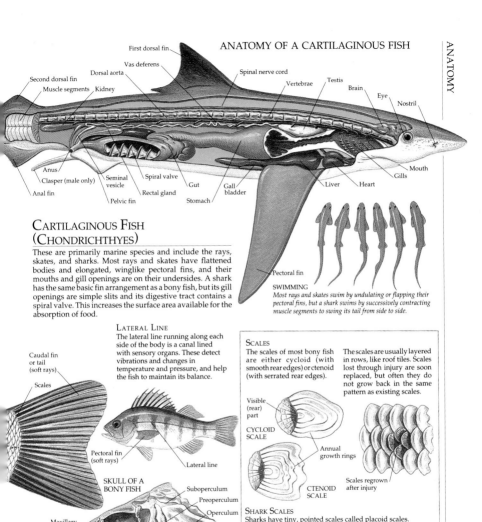

First dorsal fin
Vas deferens
Dorsal aorta
Second dorsal fin
Muscle segments   Kidney
Spinal nerve cord
Vertebrae
Testis
Brain
Eye
Nostril
Anus
Clasper (male only)   Seminal vesicle   Spiral valve
Anal fin
Rectal gland
Gut
Pelvic fin
Gall bladder
Stomach
Liver   Heart
Gills
Mouth
Pectoral fin

SWIMMING
Most rays and skates swim by undulating or flapping their pectoral fins, but a shark swims by successively contracting muscle segments to swing its tail from side to side.

CARTILAGINOUS FISH (CHONDRICHTHYES)

These are primarily marine species and include the rays, skates, and sharks. Most rays and skates have flattened bodies and elongated, winglike pectoral fins, and their mouths and gill openings are on their undersides. A shark has the same basic fin arrangement as a bony fish, but its gill openings are simple slits and its digestive tract contains a spiral valve. This increases the surface area available for the absorption of food.

LATERAL LINE
The lateral line running along each side of the body is a canal lined with sensory organs. These detect vibrations and changes in temperature and pressure, and help the fish to maintain its balance.

Caudal fin or tail (soft rays)
Scales
Pectoral fin (soft rays)
Lateral line

SKULL OF A BONY FISH
Suboperculum
Preoperculum
Operculum
Maxillary
Premaxillary
Dentary
Cleithrum
Articular
Supracleithrum
Quadrate   Introperculum

SCALES
The scales of most bony fish are either cycloid (with smooth rear edges) or ctenoid (with serrated rear edges).

The scales are usually layered in rows, like roof tiles. Scales lost through injury are soon replaced, but often they do not grow back in the same pattern as existing scales.

Visible (rear) part
CYCLOID SCALE
Annual growth rings
CTENOID SCALE
Scales regrown after injury

SHARK SCALES
Sharks have tiny, pointed scales called placoid scales.

SPOTTED DOGFISH
SMOOTHHOUND

CENTRARCHIDAE

BLACK BASS

The species collectively known as black bass include two of the most important sporting species in North America: the smallmouth bass and the largemouth bass. Black bass are the largest members of the Centrarchidae family, which also includes the bluegill, the crappies, and the sunfish (*see page 12*).

SUWANNEE BASS
Micropterus notius

SUWANNEE BASS
This small bass, which rarely exceeds 12 oz (340 g), is found in the Suwannee and Ochlockonee river drainages of Florida and Georgia. Its overall coloration is brownish, with dark markings along the back and sides; the adult male has blue cheeks, breast, and belly.

Male has blue cheeks, breast, and belly

SPOTTED BASS
This bass gets its name from the rows of small, dark spots on its pale flanks and belly. It is found mainly in the Ohio and Mississippi river systems and has two localized subspecies, the Alabama spotted bass and the Wichita spotted bass, *Micropterus punctulatus henshalli* and *M. p. wichitae*. It grows to about 5 lb (2.27 kg).

GUADALUPE BASS
The Guadalupe bass is similar to the spotted bass, but has distinctive dark bars along each side and is smaller, seldom reaching 1 lb (454 g). Its range is restricted to the Guadalupe, Colorado, Brazos, San Antonio, and Nueces river systems of central Texas.

GUADALUPE BASS
Micropterus treculi

LARGEMOUTH BASS
The largemouth bass is so named because its upper jaw extends to behind its eye; that of the smallmouth bass does not extend beyond the eye. The northern largemouth seldom exceeds 10 lb (4.54 kg), but the southern subspecies, the Florida largemouth (*M. s. floridanus*), can reach more than 20 lb (9.1 kg).

SPOTTED BASS
Micropterus punctulatus

REDEYE BASS
The red eyes and white-tipped orange caudal (tail) fin of the redeye bass make it easy to distinguish from other bass; young redeyes also have brick-red dorsal and anal fins. The redeye is one of the smaller bass species, and although it can exceed 8 lb (3.6 kg) it usually does not grow to more than about 1 lb (454 g).

REDEYE BASS
Micropterus coosae

White tip to caudal fin

FISHING NOTES

Techniques
Spinning or baitcasting with artificial lures, fly fishing, and trolling with livebaits will all prove successful.

Tackle
For lure fishing, try a 5½ to 7 ft (1.7 m to 2.1 m) spinning or baitcasting rod and a spinning or baitcaster reel with 6 to 10 lb (2.7 to 4.54 kg) mono line. A good rod to use for fly fishing is a 7 to 9 ft (2.1 to 2.7 m) bass fly rod with a fast taper, fitted with a single-action fly reel carrying a floating #7 to #9 line with a 6 to 8 lb (2.7 to 3.6 kg) leader. For trolling, use a 9 or 10 ft (2.7 or 3 m) stiff-action rod with a 2½ lb (1.1 kg) test curve, and a baitcaster reel with 10 to 20 lb (4.5 to 9.1 kg) mono line, a nylon or Dacron leader, and hook sizes 2/0 to 5/0. Use weedless hooks in very dense cover.

Bait
Black bass, being active predators that feed on a wide variety of creatures, can be tempted to strike at practically any kind of bait, either artificial or natural. Artificials such as spinners, spoons, crankbaits, surface plugs, and plastic worms are particularly effective. For fly fishing, bass bugs, streamers, and bucktails have all proved their worth; for trolling, try worms, crayfish, leeches, and minnows.

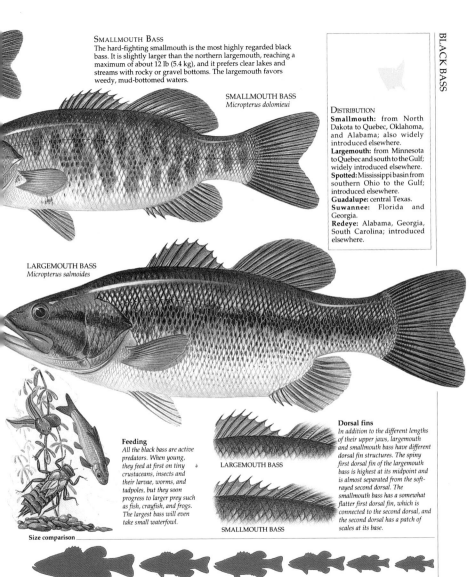

SMALLMOUTH BASS
The hard-fighting smallmouth is the most highly regarded black bass. It is slightly larger than the northern largemouth, reaching a maximum of about 12 lb (5.4 kg), and it prefers clear lakes and streams with rocky or gravel bottoms. The largemouth favors weedy, mud-bottomed waters.

SMALLMOUTH BASS
Micropterus dolomieui

LARGEMOUTH BASS
Micropterus salmoides

DISTRIBUTION
Smallmouth: from North Dakota to Quebec, Oklahoma, and Alabama; also widely introduced elsewhere.
Largemouth: from Minnesota to Quebec and south to the Gulf; widely introduced elsewhere.
Spotted: Mississippi basin from southern Ohio to the Gulf; introduced elsewhere.
Guadalupe: central Texas.
Suwannee: Florida and Georgia.
Redeye: Alabama, Georgia, South Carolina; introduced elsewhere.

Feeding
All the black bass are active predators. When young, they feed at first on tiny crustaceans, insects and their larvae, worms, and tadpoles, but they soon progress to larger prey such as fish, crayfish, and frogs. The largest bass will even take small waterfowl.

LARGEMOUTH BASS

SMALLMOUTH BASS

Dorsal fins
In addition to the different lengths of their upper jaws, largemouth and smallmouth bass have different dorsal fin structures. The spiny first dorsal fin of the largemouth bass is highest at its midpoint and is almost separated from the soft-rayed second dorsal. The smallmouth bass has a somewhat flatter first dorsal fin, which is connected to the second dorsal, and the second dorsal has a patch of scales at its base.

Size comparison

Largemouth bass   Smallmouth bass   Spotted bass   Redeye bass   Guadalupe bass   Suwannee bass

11

BLUEGILL, CRAPPIES, PUMPKINSEED, & SUNFISH

These small relatives of the black bass are among the most popular American panfish, which are fish that are too small to be considered true gamefish but still provide considerable angling (and eating) pleasure. The range of each of these species has been widely been considerably extended by widespread stocking programs.

Freshwater SPECIES

Sharply arched back and dip above eye

PUMPKINSEED
This attractive little fish lives among the weeds in lakes, ponds, and quiet river pools. Its maximum weight is about 1 lb 1 oz (482 g), but most individuals are much smaller.

BLUEGILL
This the most widely distributed panfish, and probably the most fished-for species in North America. It prefers quiet, weedy waters and averages about 4 oz (113g), although it can grow to over 4 lb (1.8 kg).

Dark spot on dorsal fin

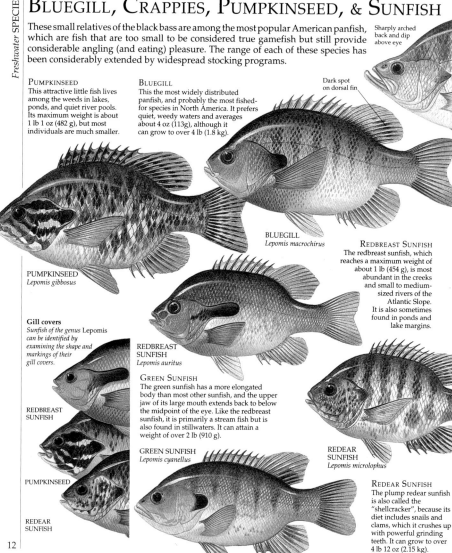

PUMPKINSEED
Lepomis gibbosus

BLUEGILL
Lepomis macrochirus

REDBREAST SUNFISH
The redbreast sunfish, which reaches a maximum weight of about 1 lb (454 g), is most abundant in the creeks and small to medium-sized rivers of the Atlantic Slope. It is also sometimes found in ponds and lake margins.

Gill covers
Sunfish of the genus Lepomis *can be identified by examining the shape and markings of their gill covers.*

REDBREAST SUNFISH

REDBREAST
SUNFISH
Lepomis auritus

GREEN SUNFISH
The green sunfish has a more elongated body than most other sunfish, and the upper jaw of its large mouth extends back to below the midpoint of the eye. Like the redbreast sunfish, it is primarily a stream fish but is also found in stillwaters. It can attain a weight of over 2 lb (910 g).

PUMPKINSEED

GREEN SUNFISH
Lepomis cyanellus

REDEAR
SUNFISH
Lepomis microlophus

REDEAR
SUNFISH

REDEAR SUNFISH
The plump redear sunfish is also called the "shellcracker", because its diet includes snails and clams, which it crushes up with powerful grinding teeth. It can grow to over 4 lb 12 oz (2.15 kg).

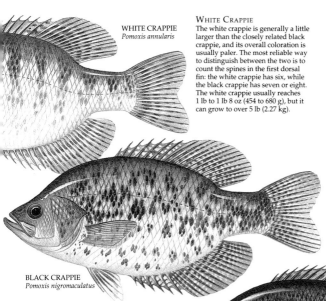

WHITE CRAPPIE
Pomoxis annularis

White Crappie

The white crappie is generally a little larger than the closely related black crappie, and its overall coloration is usually paler. The most reliable way to distinguish between the two is to count the spines in the first dorsal fin: the white crappie has six, while the black crappie has seven or eight. The white crappie usually reaches 1 lb to 1 lb 8 oz (454 to 680 g), but it can grow to over 5 lb (2.27 kg).

Distribution

Pumpkinseed: the Dakotas and Iowa to the Atlantic drainages.
Bluegill: from the Great Lakes to the Gulf and New Mexico; widely introduced elsewhere.
Redbreast sunfish: the Atlantic drainages.
Green sunfish: From the Great Lakes to Texas.
Redear sunfish: Indiana to the Gulf; introduced elsewhere.
Crappies: eastern North America from southern Canada to the Gulf; widely introduced.
Rock bass: From Manitoba to New England and northern Alabama.

BLACK CRAPPIE
Pomoxis nigromaculatus

Black Crappie

The black crappie is often found together with the white, and both species are widely distributed in ponds, lakes, and rivers, although the black tends to prefer larger, clearer waters than those tolerated by the white. Its average weight is in the 12 oz to 1 lb 8 oz (340 to 680 g) range, with a maximum of up to 5 lb (2.27 kg).

ROCK BASS
Ambloplites rupestris

Rock Bass

The mottled, dark olive rock bass has distinctive red eyes and a large mouth, and there is usually a white or gold margin to the dark spot on its gill cover. It is most common in clear, rocky streams and is also found in lake margins where the bottom is rocky and there is ample vegetation. Its maximum weight is about 1.36 kg (3 lb), but it typically weighs around 227 g (8 oz).

Fishing Notes

Techniques
Float fishing, fly fishing, and baitcasting, all with light tackle.

Tackle
For float fishing, a 10 to 14 ft (3 to 4.3 m) pole, 6 to 15 lb (2.7 to 6.8 kg) mono line, and a small jig or livebait fished below a small float; or a 6 to 7 ft (1.8 to 2.1 m) ultralight spinning rod with a spinning reel, 3 lb (1.36 kg) mono line, and a

small float. Use hook sizes 10 to 14, and weight the rig with suitable split shot about 12 in (30 cm) from the hook. For fly fishing, use a fly rod up to 4 oz (113 g) in weight, with matching reel and line. When baitcasting, use a 4½ to 6 ft (1.4 to 1.8 m) rod, a baitcasting reel, and 2 to 4 lb (910 g to 1.8 kg) line.

Bait
Small minnows, worms, grubs, and jigs for float fishing; tiny wet flies, nymphs, and dry flies for fly fishing; miniature spinners and crankbaits for baitcasting.

Size comparison

White crappie

Black crappie

Rock bass

Bluegill

Pumpkinseed

Green sunfish

Redear sunfish

Redbreast sunfish

BLUEGILL, CRAPPIES, PUMPKINSEED, & SUNFISH

13

Freshwater SPECIES

BARBEL, TENCH, & ASP

The tench is a very popular angling species in its native Eurasian waters and has been introduced into North America and Australia. It is mainly a stillwater species, although it also inhabits the lower reaches of rivers. The asp is found in large lakes and, like barbel, in the middle reaches of clean rivers where the current is relatively fast and the water well oxygenated. Asp and barbel are often found together in those areas of Europe where their ranges overlap, asp in midwater and barbel on the bottom.

FEMALE   MALE

Male and female tench
The sex of a tench can be determined from its pelvic fins. Those of the male are much longer and broader than those of the female, and they extend to beyond the anal vent.

TENCH
The tiny scales of the tench are covered with a layer of protective slime and set flat against its thick-set body, making it appear almost scaleless. The fins are smoothly rounded, and the wrist of the barely forked tail is distinctively thick. Large individuals of up to 18 lb 12 oz (8.5 kg) have been reported, but the tench is slow-growing, and the usual maximum is about 4 lb (1.8 kg).

TENCH
Tinca tinca

GOLDEN TENCH
Tinca tinca

Golden Tench
The rare golden variety of tench is stocked as an ornamental fish in private ponds and park lakes. It has an orange or yellow body with scattered black markings, and its pink-tinged fins are less rounded than those of the common tench.

Spawning male asp
At spawning time the male asp develops numerous tough, wartlike lumps (tubercles) on its head, which help it to fend off rivals. Asp spawn in spring over gravel beds.

ASP
The slender, streamlined body of the predatory asp gives it the speed and agility it needs to capture its food, which is primarily small midwater and near-surface fish. A popular angling species that fights strongly when hooked, it favors deep water and is often found in dam pools. Asp average about 7 lb 11 oz (3.5 kg), but can reach a maximum of around 26 lb 7 oz (12 kg).

Natural food
Tench and barbel have a varied diet that includes plants, insects, mollusks, and crustaceans. When young, the asp eats insects and small crustaceans, but as an adult it preys on small fish such as bleak.

ASP
Aspius aspius

Size comparison

Asp   Barbel   Tench   Southern barbel

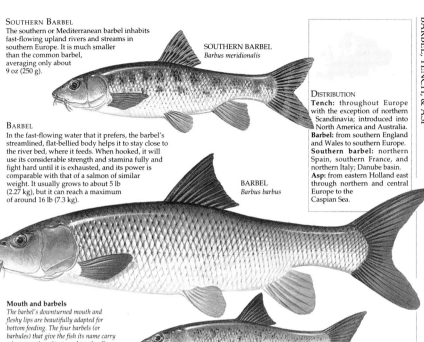

SOUTHERN BARBEL

The southern or Mediterranean barbel inhabits fast-flowing upland rivers and streams in southern Europe. It is much smaller than the common barbel, averaging only about 9 oz (250 g).

SOUTHERN BARBEL
Barbus meridionalis

BARBEL

In the fast-flowing water that it prefers, the barbel's streamlined, flat-bellied body helps it to stay close to the river bed, where it feeds. When hooked, it will use its considerable strength and stamina fully and fight hard until it is exhausted, and its power is comparable with that of a salmon of similar weight. It usually grows to about 5 lb (2.27 kg), but it can reach a maximum of around 16 lb (7.3 kg).

BARBEL
Barbus barbus

DISTRIBUTION

Tench: throughout Europe with the exception of northern Scandinavia; introduced into North America and Australia. **Barbel:** from southern England and Wales to southern Europe. **Southern barbel:** northern Spain, southern France, and northern Italy; Danube basin. **Asp:** from eastern Holland east through northern and central Europe to the Caspian Sea.

Mouth and barbels

The barbel's downturned mouth and fleshy lips are beautifully adapted for bottom feeding. The four barbels (or barbules) that give the fish its name carry a large number of taste and touch cells, and act like external tongues with which the fish can examine potential food items.

Young barbel

Up to a weight of around 8 to 12 oz (227 to 340 g) and a length of 6 to 8 in (15 to 20 cm), young barbel often have speckled flanks, and their overall coloration tends to be more olive-green than that of their parents.

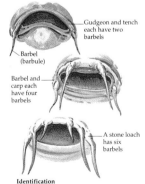

Gudgeon and tench each have two barbels

Barbel (barbule)

Barbel and carp each have four barbels

A stone loach has six barbels

Identification

Count the barbels to distinguish young barbel and carp from similar fish.

FISHING NOTES

Techniques

Float fishing, legering, and freelining for tench; lure fishing and deadbaiting for asp; for barbel, float fishing and legering, especially legering with a crankbait.

Tackle

When float fishing for tench, use a 12 ft (3.7 m) medium-action rod, a spinning reel, 10 lb (4.54 kg) line, and hook sizes 6 or 8. To leger for tench, try a 12 ft (3.7 m) Avon rod with a spinning reel, 7 lb (3.2 kg) line, size 6 to 10 hook, and a crankbait. For asp, try a 9 ft (2.7 m)

medium-action spinning rod, a spinning reel, 15 lb (6.8 kg) line, and a small spoon. To leger for barbel, use a 12 ft (3.7 m) rod with quivertip, a spinning reel, 8 lb (3.6 kg) line, hook sizes 8 to 12, and a crankbait.

Bait

Good tench baits include bread, maggots, corn, worms, meat, and small boilies. Asp can be taken on spoons, especially if a small piece of red wool is tied to the hook to provide extra attraction, and on small fish baits such as bleak. For barbel, try maggots, meat, vetches, corn, worms, bread, and cheese.

CYPRINIDAE

BREAM, NASE, & VIMBA

These European members of the carp family are all primarily bottom-feeders. Bream are widely distributed in stillwaters, canals, and deep, slow-flowing rivers; the nase prefers the faster-flowing waters of the middle reaches of rivers; and the vimba is found in the middle and lower reaches of large, slow rivers. The most wide-spread of these species, and the most popular with anglers, is the bronze bream.

YOUNG BREAM

Young bream
When young, bronze bream are silvery with black fins. In Britain, these little fish are known as tinplate bream or skimmers.

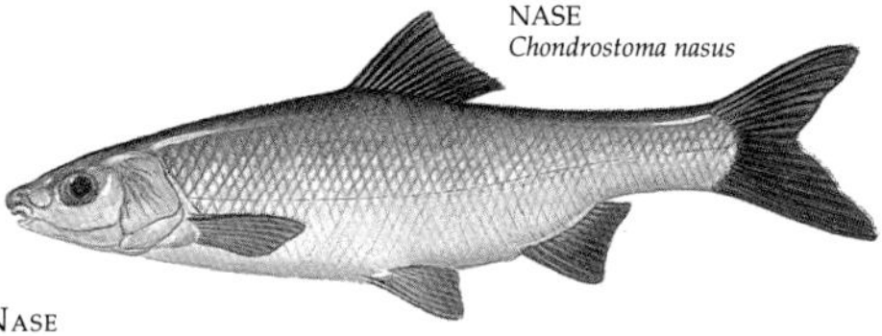

NASE
Chondrostoma nasus

Roach/bream hybrids
Where spawning schools of bream and roach (see page 21) occur in the same waters, roach/bream hybrids are common. To identify a hybrid, count the number of rays in the anal fin: a roach has 9 to 12, a bream has 23 to 29, and a hybrid 14 to 19.

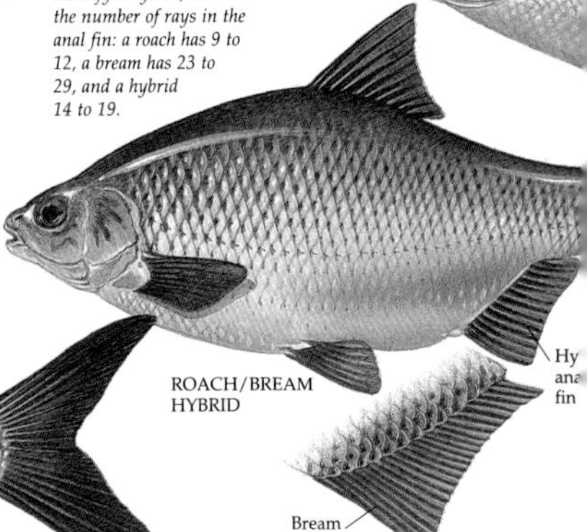

NASE
The silvery, slender-bodied nase has red-tinged fins and a smallish head with a noticeably protuberant snout. It feeds on algae and diatoms, which it scrapes from rocks and stones with its hard, horny lower lip, and can reach a maximum weight of about 4 lb (1.8 kg). The toxostome, or soiffe (*Chondrostoma toxostoma*), is similar to the nase, but smaller.

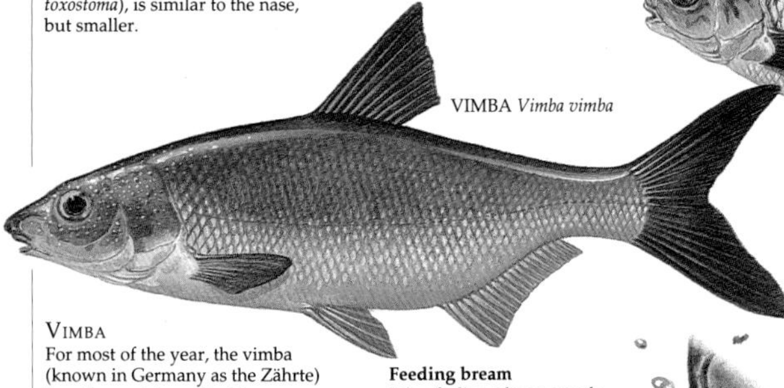

VIMBA *Vimba vimba*

ROACH/BREAM
HYBRID

Hy
ana
fin

Bream
anal fin

VIMBA
For most of the year, the vimba (known in Germany as the Zährte) has silvery sides and a blue-gray back, but at spawning time (in early summer) the male becomes very dark on the back with an orange-red belly. The vimba's staple diet consists of worms, mollusks, and crustaceans, and its weight ranges from around 2 lb (910 g) to 6 lb 10 oz (3 kg).

Feeding bream
When feeding, a bream upends itself and its mouth protrudes down to suck in worms, mollusks, crustaceans, and insect larvae. A school of feeding bream will betray its presence by stirring up clouds of silt from the bottom.

SILVER BREAM
Blicca bjoerkna

Size comparison

| Bronze bream | Vimba | Nase | Silver bream | Danubian bream |

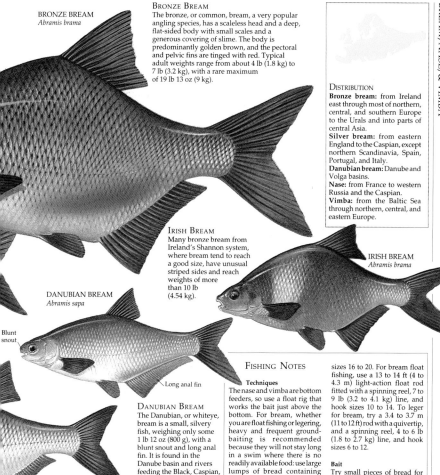

BRONZE BREAM
Abramis brama

BRONZE BREAM
The bronze, or common, bream, a very popular angling species, has a scaleless head and a deep, flat-sided body with small scales and a generous covering of slime. The body is predominantly golden brown, and the pectoral and pelvic fins are tinged with red. Typical adult weights range from about 4 lb (1.8 kg) to 7 lb (3.2 kg), with a rare maximum of 19 lb 13 oz (9 kg).

DISTRIBUTION
Bronze bream: from Ireland east through most of northern, central, and southern Europe to the Urals and into parts of central Asia.
Silver bream: from eastern England to the Caspian, except northern Scandinavia, Spain, Portugal, and Italy.
Danubian bream: Danube and Volga basins.
Nase: from France to western Russia and the Caspian.
Vimba: from the Baltic Sea through northern, central, and eastern Europe.

IRISH BREAM
Many bronze bream from Ireland's Shannon system, where bream tend to reach a good size, have unusual striped sides and reach weights of more than 10 lb (4.54 kg).

IRISH BREAM
Abramis brama

DANUBIAN BREAM
Abramis sapa

Blunt snout

Long anal fin

DANUBIAN BREAM
The Danubian, or whiteye, bream is a small, silvery fish, weighing only some 1 lb 12 oz (800 g), with a blunt snout and long anal fin. It is found in the Danube basin and rivers feeding the Black, Caspian, and Aral Seas.

FISHING NOTES
Techniques
The nase and vimba are bottom feeders, so use a float rig that works the bait just above the bottom. For bream, whether you are float fishing or legering, heavy and frequent groundbaiting is recommended because they will not stay long in a swim where there is no readily available food: use large lumps of bread containing hookbaits such as maggots, casters, or worms.

Tackle
When fishing for nase and vimba, try a 12 to 13 ft (3.7 to 4 m) float rod with a light tip action, a spinning reel, 2 lb (910 g) line, and hook sizes 16 to 20. For bream float fishing, use a 13 to 14 ft (4 to 4.3 m) light-action float rod fitted with a spinning reel, 7 to 9 lb (3.2 to 4.1 kg) line, and hook sizes 10 to 14. To leger for bream, try a 3.4 to 3.7 m (11 to 12 ft) rod with a quivertip, and a spinning reel, 4 to 6 lb (1.8 to 2.7 kg) line, and hook sizes 6 to 12.

Bait
Try small pieces of bread for nase and boiled barley, maggots, small pieces of worm, and bread for vimba. For bream, bread, maggots, casters, worms, and corn are all effective float-fishing baits, and maggots or small worms enclosed in a doughball are good for legering.

SILVER BREAM
The small size, more slender body, and brilliant silvery flanks of the silver or white bream help to distinguish it from the bronze bream. Its habitat and feeding habits are the same as those of the bronze, but it is much smaller, its usual maximum weight being only 1 lb (454 g).

17

CARP

The wild carp was being farmed for food in Asia by about 400 BC. Since then, selective breeding on eastern European fish farms has produced a number of variants such as the common, leather, and mirror forms. These and the wild carp have spread throughout Europe both naturally and by introduction, and have been introduced elsewhere, including North America and Australia.

FISHING NOTES

Techniques
Float fishing, legering, and freelining for common carp; float fishing for crucian.

Tackle
For common carp float fishing, use a 12 ft (3.7 m), 1½ lb (680 g) test curve rod with a spinning reel, 8 lb (3.6 kg) line, and hook sizes 8 to 12. Legering calls for heavier tackle, for instance a 12 ft (3.7 m), 2 lb (910 g) test curve rod with a spinning reel, 12 lb (5.4 kg) line, and hook sizes 6 to 10. For crucian carp,

use a 13 ft (4 m) light-action rod with a spinning reel, 1½ to 2½ lb (680 g to 1.1 kg) line, and hook sizes 12 to 18.

Bait
The range of baits used by carp fishermen is enormous and constantly growing. It extends from simple, traditional baits, such as bread, worms, and maggots, through luncheon meat, sweet corn, and potatoes, to the numerous commercially prepared baits such as boilies, and bait additives such as meat-, spice-, and aromatic fruit-flavored oils.

WILD CARP
The wild carp is a strong, slow-growing fish with a scaleless head and a fully scaled body. Smaller and less deep-bodied than the common carp, its average weight is 2 to 5 lb (910 g to 2.27 kg) and it seldom exceeds 20 lb (9.1 kg).

WILD CARP
Cyprinus carpio

Breeding
Wild and common carp spawn in late spring and early summer, when the water temperature exceeds 64°F (18°C). The eggs are laid in shallow water that has abundant dense vegetation and good exposure to sunlight, and are attached to the leaves and stems of water plants. They hatch in five to eight days, the hatchlings initially remaining attached to the plants. The young fish grow very quickly.

Eggs

Hatchling

Larva

Feeding
The common carp feeds at the surface, on the bottom, or in midwater on plants, algae, snails, worms, insect larvae, shrimps, mussels, and many other organisms. It opens its mouth wide and sucks its food in like a vacuum cleaner, and often rummages through the bottom detritus, sending up clouds of silt and uprooting plants.

CRUCIAN CARP
Carassius carassius

CRUCIAN CARP
This small, deep-bodied carp is more closely related to the goldfish than to the wild carp, but will interbreed with both species. It averages about 9 oz (255 g), but can exceed 5 lb 8 oz (2.5 kg), and it will tolerate a wide range of temperatures, low oxygen levels, acidity, and dense vegetation.

Size comparison

| Grass carp | Common carp | Mirror carp | Leather carp | Wild carp | Crucian carp | Goldfish |

GRASS CARP

The wide mouth of the grass carp is superbly adapted for feeding on plants, and because of its huge appetite it has been introduced into many canals, ponds, and drains in Europe and North America for weed clearance. Its growth rate is very rapid, and in warm waters it can reach 77 lb (35 kg).

GRASS CARP
Ctenopharyngodon idella

GOLDFISH
Carassius auratus

DISTRIBUTION

Common carp: through most of Eurasia; North America, South Africa, India, Australia, and New Zealand.
Crucian, grass, and goldfish: native to Eurasia and widely introduced elsewhere.

GOLDFISH

Within a few generations of release into the wild, the domestic goldfish reverts to its natural carplike coloration and can grow to a weight of about 6lb 10 oz (3 kg).

COMMON (OR KING) CARP

The heavy, deep-bodied common, or king, carp, together with its leather and mirror varieties, is the result of centuries of selective breeding by fish farms. Like the wild carp from which it derives, the common carp has a scaleless head and a fully scaled body, and its coloration is variable. It can reach a weight of 80 lb (36 kg) and a length of about 5 ft (1.5 m).

COMMON (OR KING) CARP
Cyprinus carpio

Mirror carp scale
The scales of the mirror carp are much larger than those of the common carp. A typical mirror carp scale might be 2 in (5 cm) long and 1.2 in (3 cm) wide, compared with a length of 1.2 in (3 cm) and a width of 1 in (2.5 cm) for a scale of a similar-sized common carp.

MIRROR CARP
Cyprinus carpio

LEATHER CARP

The scaleless or almost-scaleless leather carp is a variety of common carp. Any scales that are present are large and few in number, and usually near the fins and tail. Like the common and mirror varieties, it has been introduced around the world.

LEATHER CARP
Cyprinus carpio

MIRROR CARP

The mirror variety of common carp occurs in a number of forms. The fully scaled is covered in large, irregular scales; the scattered has individual, randomly sited scales; the linear has a continuous line of scales along the lateral line; and the plated has just a few, very large, scales along the lateral line.

CYPRINIDAE

CHUB, DACE, ROACH, & RUDD

These popular angling species are widespread in the rivers and
stillwaters of Europe. Chub and dace prefer moderate to fast flows
of clean water, but they are also found in slow lowland rivers and
sometimes in lakes. Roach and rudd thrive in canals, slow-flowing
rivers, and stillwaters where there is plenty of vegetation. The roach
has been introduced into Australia, where it is found in Victoria and
southern New South Wales, and the rudd has been
introduced into the northeastern United States,
where there are breeding populations in Maine
and in the lower Hudson basin in New York.

Chub food
*Young chub eat mostly
insect larvae and aquatic
invertebrates. Adults will take
anything edible that comes their way,
opening their large, wide mouths to
engulf small fish, frogs, crayfish, and small
water voles, and snapping up berries that fall
from overhanging trees and bushes.*

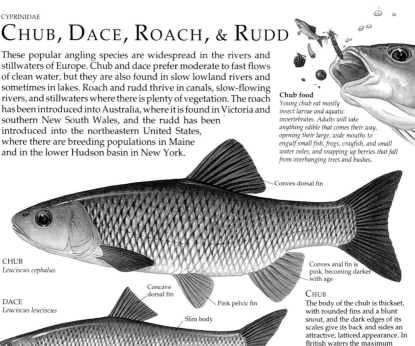

Convex dorsal fin

CHUB
Leuciscus cephalus

Convex anal fin is
pink, becoming darker
with age

Concave
dorsal fin

DACE
Leuciscus leuciscus

Pink pelvic fin

Slim body

CHUB
The body of the chub is thickset,
with rounded fins and a blunt
snout, and the dark edges of its
scales give its back and sides an
attractive, latticed appearance. In
British waters the maximum
weight is probably about 12 lb
(5.4 kg), but in mainland Europe it
can reach 16 lb (7.26 kg).

Concave anal fin

DACE
The slim, silvery dace is one of
the smallest species to be of serious
angling interest: its maximum weight is only about 1 lb 5 oz
(600 g), and a fish of 6 to 8 oz (170 to 227 g) would be a
good catch. It feeds on insects, crustaceans, and plants.

Protruding
lower
jaw

Large eye

BLEAK
Alburnus alburnus

Long anal fin

FISHING NOTES

Techniques
Float fishing and legering are
the most usual techniques for
these species, but fly fishing is
an enjoyable alternative.

Tackle
To leger for chub, use a 12 ft
(3.7 m) rod with a built-in
quivertip, and a spinning reel,
5 lb (2.27 kg) line, hook sizes 8
to 16, and a suitable blockend

crankbait. For float fishing, try
a 12 to 13 ft (3.7 to 4 m) rod with
a spinning reel, 3 lb (1.36 kg)
line, and hook sizes 14 to 20. To
float fish for dace, use a 12 ft
(3.7 m) rod with a light tip action, a spinning reel, 2 lb (910 g)
line, and hook sizes 16 to 20. To
float fish for roach or rudd, try
a 12 ft (3.7 m) rod with a light
action, a spinning reel, 2½ lb
(1.1 kg) line, and hook sizes
14 to 20. When legering for
roach or rudd, use a 10 to 12 ft

(3 to 3.7 m) rod with quivertip,
a spinning reel, 2½ to 4 lb (1.36
to 1.8 kg) line, and hook sizes
10 to 16.

Bait
For all these species, good float
fishing or legering baits include
maggots, casters, bread, and
worms, and large slugs are
especially effective for chub.
These species can also be taken
on fly tackle, using either wet
or dry flies.

Chub, dace, or bleak?
*Young chub are similar in size and
general appearance to dace and
bleak, but each has its own
distinguishing features. The chub
has convex dorsal and anal fins,
and its pelvic and anal fins are
pink. In comparison, the grayish
dorsal fin and pale, yellowish anal
fins of the dace are concave, and
the grayish, concave anal fin of the
bleak is much longer than that of
either the chub or the dace. The
bleak also has a protruding lower
jaw and large, prominent eyes.*

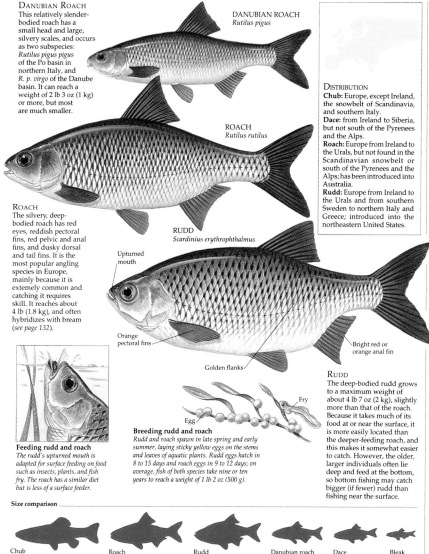

DANUBIAN ROACH
This relatively slender-bodied roach has a small head and large, silvery scales, and occurs as two subspecies: *Rutilus pigus pigus* of the Po basin in northern Italy, and *R. p. virgo* of the Danube basin. It can reach a weight of 2 lb 3 oz (1 kg) or more, but most are much smaller.

DANUBIAN ROACH
Rutilus pigus

ROACH
Rutilus rutilus

ROACH
The silvery, deep-bodied roach has red eyes, reddish pectoral fins, red pelvic and anal fins, and dusky dorsal and tail fins. It is the most popular angling species in Europe, mainly because it is extremely common and catching it requires skill. It reaches about 4 lb (1.8 kg), and often hybridizes with bream (*see page 132*).

RUDD
Scardinius erythrophthalmus

Upturned mouth

Orange pectoral fins

Golden flanks

Bright red or orange anal fin

DISTRIBUTION
Chub: Europe, except Ireland, the snowbelt of Scandinavia, and southern Italy.
Dace: from Ireland to Siberia, but not south of the Pyrenees and the Alps.
Roach: Europe from Ireland to the Urals, but not found in the Scandinavian snowbelt or south of the Pyrenees or the Alps; has been introduced into Australia.
Rudd: Europe from Ireland to the Urals and from southern Sweden to northern Italy and Greece; introduced into the northeastern United States.

Feeding rudd and roach
The rudd's upturned mouth is adapted for surface feeding on food such as insects, plants, and fish fry. The roach has a similar diet but is less of a surface feeder.

Fry

Egg

Breeding rudd and roach
Rudd and roach spawn in late spring and early summer, laying sticky yellow eggs on the stems and leaves of aquatic plants. Rudd eggs hatch in 8 to 15 days and roach eggs in 9 to 12 days; on average, fish of both species take nine or ten years to reach a weight of 1 lb 2 oz (500 g).

RUDD
The deep-bodied rudd grows to a maximum weight of about 4 lb 7 oz (2 kg), slightly more than that of the roach. Because it takes much of its food at or near the surface, it is more easily located than the deeper-feeding roach, and this makes it somewhat easier to catch. However, the older, larger individuals often lie deep and feed at the bottom, so bottom fishing may catch bigger (if fewer) rudd than fishing near the surface.

Size comparison

Chub   Roach   Rudd   Danubian roach   Dace   Bleak

ESOCIDAE

PIKE, PICKEREL, & MUSKELLUNGE

The members of the pike family are voracious predators, disliked and even feared by some anglers but greatly admired by others because of their size and the tenacious fight they put up when hooked. They inhabit rivers, streams, and stillwaters with clear water but with plenty of vegetation in which to lurk in wait for their prey. The pike itself, known in North America as the northern pike, is one of the few freshwater species native to both Eurasia and North America. Pickerel and muskellunge are purely North American species.

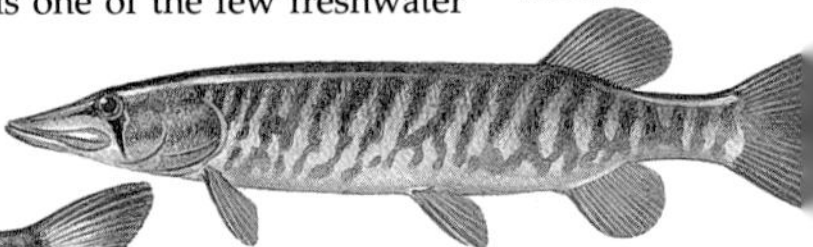

REDFIN PICKEREL
Esox americanus americanus

GRASS PICKEREL
Esox americanus vermiculatus

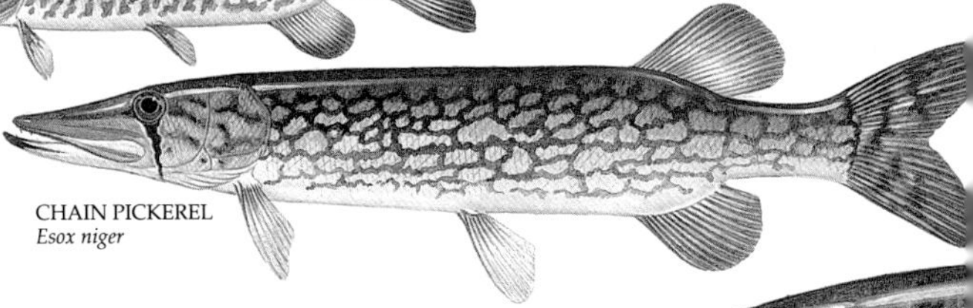

PICKEREL

The chain pickerel averages only 2 lb (910 g) but has been known to reach 9 lb 6 oz (4.25 kg). Despite being relatively small, it provides good sport on light tackle, as do the even smaller grass and redfin pickerels, which are less than half its size. Apart from the difference in their sizes, the chain pickerel can be distinguished from the grass and redfin by its markings. The chain pickerel has a distinctive dark, chainlike pattern on its sides, while the grass and redfin are both marked with dark bars; the redfin, as its name implies, also has red fins.

CHAIN PICKEREL
Esox niger

MUSKELLUNGE

The mighty muskellunge is a powerful, fast-growing fish that can reach a length of 12 in (30 cm) in only four months and grows to 6 ft (1.83 m) or more. Its maximum weight is at least 70 lb (31.75 kg), and weights in excess of 100 lb (45 kg) have been reported. The most visible difference between the muskellunge and the northern pike is in their markings: the "muskie" has dark bars or blotches on its sides, while the pike has a series of pale bars and spots.

MUSKELLUNGE
Esox masquinongy

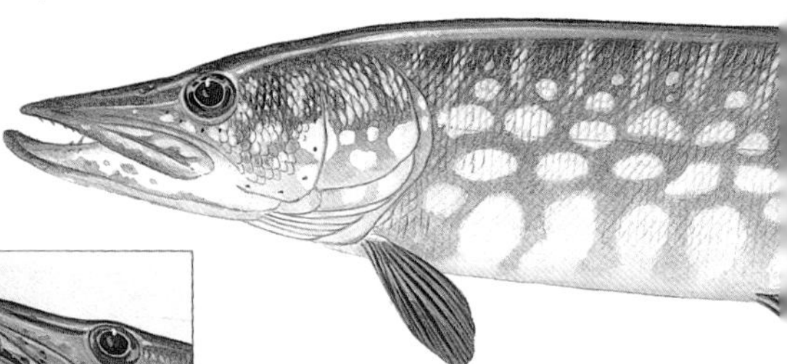

FEEDING

The principal food of the pike family is fish, including smaller fish of their own kind. They are, however, great opportunists and will take any available small prey including frogs, snakes, crayfish, rodents, and ducklings. Their markings provide excellent camouflage as they hide among the weeds, waiting to pounce on passing fish, which they swallow head first.

FISHING NOTES

Techniques
These active predators are usually caught by spinning, baitcasting, and trolling, using lures, deadbaits, and livebaits. Fish for them from the bank, or use a boat to reach weedbeds that are otherwise inaccessible.

Tackle
For pickerel, try a 5½ ft (1.7 m) baitcaster with a baitcaster reel or a 6 to 7 ft (1.8 to 2.1 m) spinning rod with a spinning reel; use 6 to 8 lb (2.7 to 3.6 kg) line with a short wire leader. When lure fishing from the bank or a boat for pike or muskellunge, try a 6 to 9 ft (1.8 to 2.7 m) spinning or baitcasting rod with a baitcaster or a spinning reel, 10 to 15 lb (4.54 to 6.8 kg) line, and a 20 lb (9.1 kg) wire leader. When you are downrigger trolling for pike or muskellunge, use a 6 to 7 ft (1.8 to 2.1 m) fast-taper rod with a baitcaster reel, 15 to 20 lb (6.8 to 9.1 kg) line, and a 25 lb (11.3 kg) wire leader.

Bait
Small spinners and spoons are ideal baits for pickerel. For pike and muskellunge, use large spinners, spoons, and plugs, cut fish baits (especially herring, mackerel, and eel), and whole minnows.

DISTRIBUTION
Pike: northern Europe south to the Pyrenees, east to Siberia; Labrador west to Alaska, south to Pennsylvania, Missouri, and Nebraska.
Muskellunge: Great Lakes region, Mississippi basin, Atlantic drainages south to Georgia and Virginia.
Chain pickerel: Atlantic drainages from Nova Scotia to Florida, Mississippi basin from Missouri south.
Redfin pickerel: Atlantic drainages.
Grass pickerel: Mississippi basin and Great Lakes.

Jaws
The members of the pike family have abundant sharp teeth and very complex skull and jaw structures. These enable them to seize and swallow relatively large fish and other prey; the pike, for example, tends to select prey that is 10 to 25 percent of its own body weight.

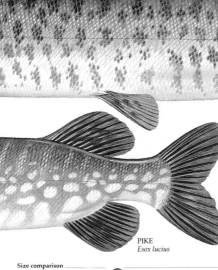

NORTHERN PIKE
Like the other members of the family, the pike is an aggressive, solitary hunter, and its torpedo-shaped body is built for short bursts of acceleration rather than sustained speed. It is usually found in or near weedbeds that provide it with cover, but in large lakes it ventures into open water to feed on salmon, trout, or other fish. Growth rates for pike vary enormously and are directly dependent on the available food supply, but an annual weight gain of 2 to 3 lb (910 g to 1.4 kg) is fairly typical. The maximum weight is thought to be about 75 lb (34 kg), but most are much smaller and a pike of 10 to 20 lb (4.54 to 9.1 kg) is a worthwhile catch.

PIKE
Esox lucius

Size comparison

Muskellunge
Northern pike
Chain pickerel
Grass pickerel
Redfin pickerel

23

ICTALURIDAE

BULLHEAD

The North American bullhead and freshwater catfish (*see page 26*) are members of the Ictaluridae, which, with some 40 species, is the largest family of freshwater fish native to North America; some have been introduced into Europe and elsewhere. Bullhead are omnivorous, bottom-feeding fish, found mostly in still and slow-flowing waters and characterized by a scaleless body, four pairs of barbels, and adipose fin, and stiff, sharp spines at the leading edges of the pectoral and dorsal fins.

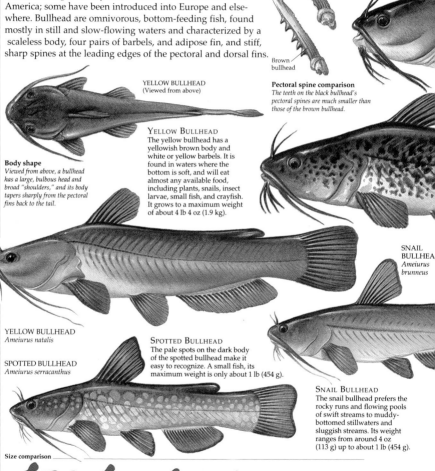

PECTORAL SPINES

Black bullhead

Brown bullhead

Pectoral spine comparison
The teeth on the black bullhead's pectoral spines are much smaller than those of the brown bullhead.

YELLOW BULLHEAD
(Viewed from above)

YELLOW BULLHEAD
The yellow bullhead has a yellowish brown body and white or yellow barbels. It is found in waters where the bottom is soft, and will eat almost any available food, including plants, snails, insect larvae, small fish, and crayfish. It grows to a maximum weight of about 4 lb 4 oz (1.9 kg).

Body shape
Viewed from above, a bullhead has a large, bulbous head and broad "shoulders," and its body tapers sharply from the pectoral fins back to the tail.

SNAIL BULLHEAD
Ameiurus brunneus

YELLOW BULLHEAD
Ameiurus natalis

SPOTTED BULLHEAD
Ameiurus serracanthus

SPOTTED BULLHEAD
The pale spots on the dark body of the spotted bullhead make it easy to recognize. A small fish, its maximum weight is only about 1 lb (454 g).

SNAIL BULLHEAD
The snail bullhead prefers the rocky runs and flowing pools of swift streams to muddy-bottomed stillwaters and sluggish streams. Its weight ranges from around 4 oz (113 g) up to about 1 lb (454 g).

Size comparison

Black bullhead   Brown bullhead   Yellow bullhead   Snail bullhead   Flat bullhead   Spotted bullhead

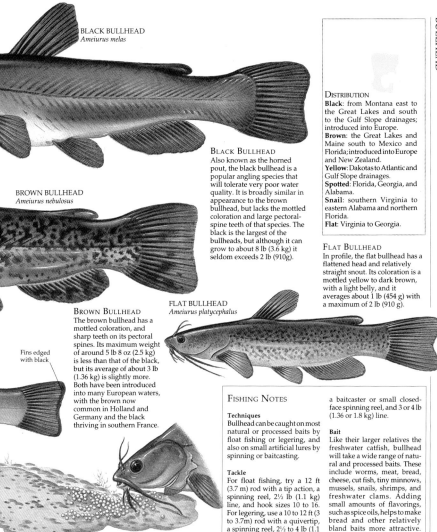

BLACK BULLHEAD
Ameiurus melas

BROWN BULLHEAD
Ameiurus nebulosus

DISTRIBUTION
Black: from Montana east to the Great Lakes and south to the Gulf Slope drainages; introduced into Europe.
Brown: the Great Lakes and Maine south to Mexico and Florida; introduced into Europe and New Zealand.
Yellow: Dakotas to Atlantic and Gulf Slope drainages.
Spotted: Florida, Georgia, and Alabama.
Snail: southern Virginia to eastern Alabama and northern Florida.
Flat: Virginia to Georgia.

BLACK BULLHEAD
Also known as the horned pout, the black bullhead is a popular angling species that will tolerate very poor water quality. It is broadly similar in appearance to the brown bullhead, but lacks the mottled coloration and large pectoral-spine teeth of that species. The black is the largest of the bullheads, but although it can grow to about 8 lb (3.6 kg) it seldom exceeds 2 lb (910g).

FLAT BULLHEAD
In profile, the flat bullhead has a flattened head and relatively straight snout. Its coloration is a mottled yellow to dark brown, with a light belly, and it averages about 1 lb (454 g) with a maximum of 2 lb (910 g).

FLAT BULLHEAD
Ameiurus platycephalus

BROWN BULLHEAD
The brown bullhead has a mottled coloration, and sharp teeth on its pectoral spines. Its maximum weight of around 5 lb 8 oz (2.5 kg) is less than that of the black, but its average of about 3 lb (1.36 kg) is slightly more. Both have been introduced into many European waters, with the brown now common in Holland and Germany and the black thriving in southern France.

Fins edged with black

Spawning bullhead
Bullhead spawn in spring and early summer, laying their eggs in depressions in the mud or among stones or other cover. One or both parents will then guard the eggs until they hatch.

FISHING NOTES

Techniques
Bullhead can be caught on most natural or processed baits by float fishing or legering, and also on small artificial lures by spinning or baitcasting.

Tackle
For float fishing, try a 12 ft (3.7 m) rod with a tip action, a spinning reel, 2½ lb (1.1 kg) line, and hook sizes 10 to 16. For legering, use a 10 to 12 ft (3 to 3.7m) rod with a quivertip, a spinning reel, 2½ to 4 lb (1.1 to 1.8 kg) line, and hook sizes 10 to 16. For spinning or baitcasting, try a 5 to 7 ft (1.5 to 2.1 m) medium-action rod with a baitcaster or small closed-face spinning reel, and 3 or 4 lb (1.36 or 1.8 kg) line.

Bait
Like their larger relatives the freshwater catfish, bullhead will take a wide range of natural and processed baits. These include worms, meat, bread, cheese, cut fish, tiny minnows, mussels, snails, shrimps, and freshwater clams. Adding small amounts of flavorings, such as spice oils, helps to make bread and other relatively bland baits more attractive. When baitcasting or spinning, try lightweight spinners and spoons, plastic worms, tiny jigs, and small wet flies.

Freshwater SPECIES

FRESHWATER CATFISH

Worldwide, there are over 30 families of freshwater and marine catfish, containing about 2,250 species. These families include the Ictaluridae of North America (*see also page 24*), the Siluridae of Europe, and the Plotosidae of Australasia, all of which have scaleless bodies, broad heads, and "whiskers" around their mouths. They generally inhabit still or slow-flowing waters, and are most active at night and on cloudy days.

Head shows distinctive flattening

YOUNG ADULT FISH

CHANNEL CATFISH
Ictalurus punctatus

CHANNEL CATFISH
The channel catfish, one of the larger North American catfish species, is the only one to have both spots and a deeply forked tail; the spots tend to fade in old, large fish. Its maximum size is about 60 lb (27 kg).

WHITE CATFISH
The coloration of the white catfish varies from white to silvery beige or blue, with a white belly. It is very popular as an angling and food fish, and usually grows to about 3 lb (1.36 kg) although it has been known to reach weights of over 17 lb (7.7 kg).

WELS
Also known as the Danubian catfish, the wels is native to central and eastern Europe but has been widely introduced into western European waters. The reason for these introductions is that the wels is one of the largest of all freshwater fish, reliably known to reach a length of 9 ft 10 in (3 m) and a weight of 441 lb (200 kg); individuals weighing over 700 lb (320 kg) have been reported.

WELS
Silurus glanis

WHITE CATFISH
Ameiurus catus

TANDAN
Tandanus tandanus

TANDAN
The tandan is a member of the Plotosidae family, which comprises about 30 marine and freshwater species that are widely distributed throughout Australasia and the Indo-Pacific. It inhabits stillwaters and slow-flowing streams, typically reaching a weight of up to 4 lb 7 oz (2 kg) with a maximum of about 13 lb 4 oz (6 kg).

FISHING NOTES

Techniques
Freshwater catfish are usually taken on natural or processed baits by float fishing, legering, or freelining, but spinning with artificial lures is also effective, particularly for channel and blue catfish.

Tackle
Use a 9 to 10 ft (2.7 to 3m) rod, such as a heavy bass rod, with a spinning reel, 6 to 12 lb (2.7 to 5.4 kg) line, and hook sizes 6 to 1/0. To freeline for the larger species, such as the wels, use a 10 to 12 ft (3 to 3.7 m) rod with a powerful action, a spinning reel, 15 lb (6.8 kg) line, 20 lb (9.1 kg) Dacron leader, and hook sizes 4 to 2/0.

Bait
Freshwater catfish can be taken on practically any type of bait or lure, even a bare, shiny hook. Every catfish angler has a personal preference when it comes to a choice of bait, but the best results are said to come with "stink" baits. These baits include soured clams and ripened chicken entrails, beef liver, pig liver, and rabbit liver, coagulated blood, and even pieces of scented soap.

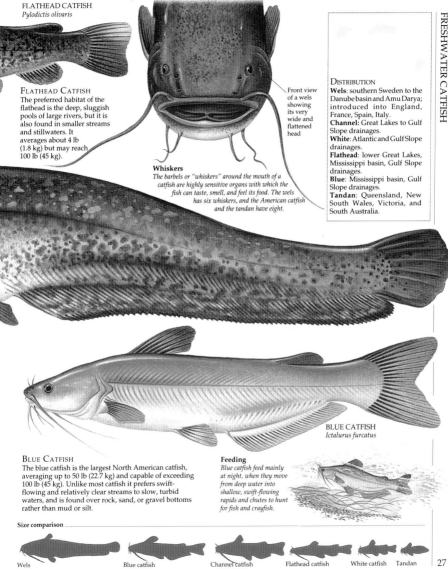

FLATHEAD CATFISH
Pylodictis olivaris

FLATHEAD CATFISH
The preferred habitat of the flathead is the deep, sluggish pools of large rivers, but it is also found in smaller streams and stillwaters. It averages about 4 lb (1.8 kg) but may reach 100 lb (45 kg).

Front view of a wels showing its very wide and flattened head

Whiskers
The barbels or "whiskers" around the mouth of a catfish are highly sensitive organs with which the fish can taste, smell, and feel its food. The wels has six whiskers, and the American catfish and the tandan have eight.

DISTRIBUTION
Wels: southern Sweden to the Danube basin and Amu Darya; introduced into England, France, Spain, Italy.
Channel: Great Lakes to Gulf Slope drainages.
White: Atlantic and Gulf Slope drainages.
Flathead: lower Great Lakes, Mississippi basin, Gulf Slope drainages.
Blue: Mississippi basin, Gulf Slope drainages.
Tandan: Queensland, New South Wales, Victoria, and South Australia.

BLUE CATFISH
Ictalurus furcatus

BLUE CATFISH
The blue catfish is the largest North American catfish, averaging up to 50 lb (22.7 kg) and capable of exceeding 100 lb (45 kg). Unlike most catfish it prefers swift-flowing and relatively clear waters, and is found over rock, sand, or gravel bottoms rather than mud or silt.

Feeding
Blue catfish feed mainly at night, when they move from deep water into shallow, swift-flowing rapids and chutes to hunt for fish and crayfish.

Size comparison

| Wels | Blue catfish | Channel catfish | Flathead catfish | White catfish | Tandan |

27

BASS & MURRAY COD

Until recently, these perchlike species were all classified as members of the Percichthyidae family, but those of the genus *Morone* are now considered to be a separate family, the Moronidae. Both families are widely distributed in temperate and tropical waters, some being exclusively freshwater fish, others exclusively marine, and some migrating from the sea into freshwater to spawn. They feed mainly on small fish, crustaceans, worms, and insects.

AUSTRALIAN BASS

This is one of the most important gamefish of the coastal rivers, estuaries, and lakes of southeastern Australia. It grows to a weight of 2 lb 3 oz (1 kg) or more, and spawns in estuaries during the winter. The eggs hatch in about three days, and by around three months of age, the young fish resemble small adults but are marked with faint vertical bars on the back and sides.

AUSTRALIAN BASS
Macquaria novemaculeata

YELLOW BASS
Morone mississippiensis

WHITE PERCH
Morone americana

WHITE PERCH

The white perch can reach a weight of about 4 lb 12 oz (2.2 kg), but averages only about 1 lb (454 g). It is found in the Atlantic Slope drainages of northeastern North America, primarily in brackish water near the mouths of rivers. It is also found in the quiet pools of medium to large rivers, and close inshore in shallow coastal waters.

YELLOW BASS

This little freshwater bass has silvery yellow sides, and the lower stripes along them are broken and offset. It rarely exceeds 2 lb 3 oz (1 kg) and usually weighs only 4 to 12 oz (113 to 340 g), but despite its small size it offers good sport on light tackle.

WHITE BASS
Morone chrysops

WHITE BASS

The white bass is very similar to the yellow bass, but its coloration is silvery white, the stripes along its sides are not broken and offset, and its lower jaw is more protuberant. It is found mainly in large, relatively clear waters, and although it grows to over 6 lb 10 oz (3 kg) most of those caught are in the 8 oz to 2 lb (227 to 910 g) range.

Size comparison

Striped bass   Murray cod   European sea bass Spotted sea bass Australian bass Yellow bass White bass White perch

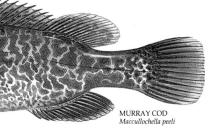

MURRAY COD

With a maximum length of 6 ft (1.8 m) and a weight of up to 250 lb (113.5 kg), the Murray cod is the largest Australian freshwater fish. Its preferred habitat is deep holes in muddy, slow-flowing water, and it is fished for commercially as well as for sport. It is widely distributed through the Murray-Darling River system, and has been introduced into many lakes in New South Wales and Victoria.

MURRAY COD
Maccullochella peeli

SPOTTED SEA BASS
Dicentrarchus punctatus

EUROPEAN SEA BASS
Dicentrarchus labrax

STRIPED BASS
Morone saxatilis

DISTRIBUTION

Australian bass, Murray cod: Queensland to Victoria.
White perch: from Quebec to South Carolina.
Yellow bass: from Montana and Wisconsin south to the Gulf of Mexico.
White bass: Manitoba and Quebec to the Gulf.
Spotted sea bass: western France to North Africa.
European sea bass: southern Norway to the Black Sea.

SPOTTED SEA BASS

The spotted sea bass is similar in size and habits to the European sea bass, from which it may be distinguished by its spotted sides. Its range overlaps that of the European sea bass, but it is not found as far north.

EUROPEAN SEA BASS

The European sea bass is found in coastal waters and the brackish water of estuaries, and reaches a weight of about 19 lb (8.6 kg). It spawns in the sea in spring and early summer, and young fish often have spots on their sides like those of the spotted bass; these spots fade and disappear as the fish mature.

STRIPED BASS

This large bass, which can grow to 6 ft 7 in (2 m) long and a weight of 126 lb (57 kg), is found along the Atlantic and Gulf coasts of North America, and was introduced into the Pacific coastal waters in 1886. It migrates into freshwater to spawn during late spring and early summer, and there are a number of landlocked, lake-dwelling populations. It will readily take baits such as mullet, sandeels, squid, crabs, clams, worms, and lures, and is fished for commercially as well as for sport.

FISHING NOTES

Techniques
In freshwater, try spinning or trolling for striped bass and Murray cod, and spinning or fly fishing for the smaller species. In saltwater, try surfcasting, trolling, or uptide fishing.

Tackle
For freshwater striped bass and Murray cod, use a heavy spinning rod with 20 to 40 lb (9.1 to 18.1 kg) line. For the smaller freshwater fish, use a 7 to 9 ft (2.1 to 2.7 m) light spinning or fly rod. For striped bass in saltwater, try a 30 lb (13.6 kg) class boat rod for trolling and a 12 ft (3.7 m) rod for surfcasting; when fishing for the smaller species in saltwater, use an 11 ft (3.4 m) light surfcasting rod or a 12 lb (5.4 kg) class uptide rod.

Bait
These fish are all active predators, and will therefore take most suitably sized natural baits or artificial lures.

Freshwater SPECIES

AUSTRALIAN PERCH & GRUNTERS

The Macquarie, golden, and estuary perches are members of the Percichthyidae family (*see page 28*), while the jungle perch belongs to the Kuhliidae, a small family of fish that are similar to the Centrarchidae of North America (*see pages 10–13*). The silver perch and sooty grunter are members of the Teraponidae (grunter) family, which consists of about 45 Indo-Pacific marine and freshwater species.

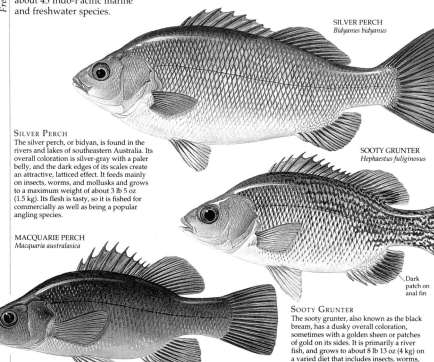

SILVER PERCH
Bidyanus bidyanus

SOOTY GRUNTER
Hephaestus fuliginosus

Dark patch on anal fin

MACQUARIE PERCH
Macquaria australasica

Elongated rays

SILVER PERCH
The silver perch, or bidyan, is found in the rivers and lakes of southeastern Australia. Its overall coloration is silver-gray with a paler belly, and the dark edges of its scales create an attractive, latticed effect. It feeds mainly on insects, worms, and mollusks, and grows to a maximum weight of about 3 lb 5 oz (1.5 kg). Its flesh is tasty, so it is fished for commercially as well as being a popular angling species.

SOOTY GRUNTER
The sooty grunter, also known as the black bream, has a dusky overall coloration, sometimes with a golden sheen or patches of gold on its sides. It is primarily a river fish, and grows to about 8 lb 13 oz (4 kg) on a varied diet that includes insects, worms, shrimps, frogs, and berries.

MACQUARIE PERCH
The color of the Macquarie perch varies from greenish brown to almost black, with a pale, sometimes yellowish, belly. It occurs in cool rivers and deep lakes, and has been introduced into reservoirs. Its diet consists mainly of insects, mollusks, and crustaceans, and it reaches a weight of around 3 lb 5 oz (1.5 kg). It spawns in spring and early summer.

FISHING NOTES

Techniques
Spinning or baitcasting with artificial lures, fly fishing, and trolling with livebaits will all prove successful.

Tackle
For lure fishing, try a 2.1 m (7 ft) spinning or baitcasting rod, a spinning or baitcaster reel and 6 lb (2.7 kg) mono line. For fly fishing, use a 9 ft (2.7 m) rod with a fast taper, a fly reel, and a floating #7 to #9 line with a 6 lb (2.7 kg) leader. For trolling, use a 9 ft (2.7 m) stiff-action rod with a 2½ lb (1.1 kg) test curve, and a baitcaster reel with 10 to 20 lb (4.54 to 9.1 kg) mono line, a nylon or Dacron leader attached by a swivel, and hook sizes 2/0 to 5/0.

Bait
These fish will take a wide range of lures and flies, and trolled natural baits such as worms, minnows, and crayfish.

30

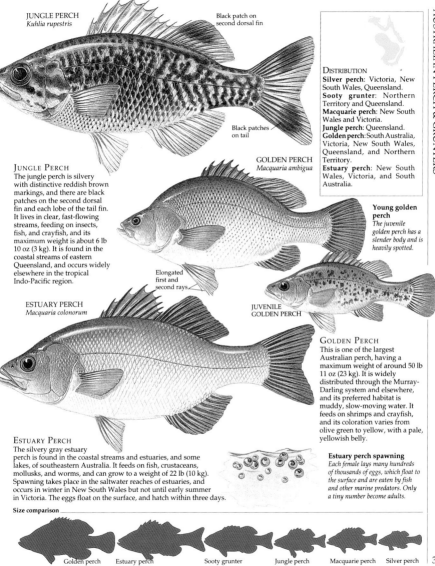

JUNGLE PERCH
Kuhlia rupestris

Black patch on second dorsal fin

Black patches on tail

JUNGLE PERCH

The jungle perch is silvery with distinctive reddish brown markings, and there are black patches on the second dorsal fin and each lobe of the tail fin. It lives in clear, fast-flowing streams, feeding on insects, fish, and crayfish, and its maximum weight is about 6 lb 10 oz (3 kg). It is found in the coastal streams of eastern Queensland, and occurs widely elsewhere in the tropical Indo-Pacific region.

GOLDEN PERCH
Macquaria ambigua

DISTRIBUTION
Silver perch: Victoria, New South Wales, Queensland.
Sooty grunter: Northern Territory and Queensland.
Macquarie perch: New South Wales and Victoria.
Jungle perch: Queensland.
Golden perch: South Australia, Victoria, New South Wales, Queensland, and Northern Territory.
Estuary perch: New South Wales, Victoria, and South Australia.

Young golden perch
The juvenile golden perch has a slender body and is heavily spotted.

ESTUARY PERCH
Macquaria colonorum

Elongated first and second rays

JUVENILE
GOLDEN PERCH

GOLDEN PERCH

This is one of the largest Australian perch, having a maximum weight of around 50 lb 11 oz (23 kg). It is widely distributed through the Murray-Darling system and elsewhere, and its preferred habitat is muddy, slow-moving water. It feeds on shrimps and crayfish, and its coloration varies from olive green to yellow, with a pale, yellowish belly.

ESTUARY PERCH

The silvery gray estuary perch is found in the coastal streams and estuaries, and some lakes, of southeastern Australia. It feeds on fish, crustaceans, mollusks, and worms, and can grow to a weight of 22 lb (10 kg). Spawning takes place in the saltwater reaches of estuaries, and occurs in winter in New South Wales but not until early summer in Victoria. The eggs float on the surface, and hatch within three days.

Estuary perch spawning
Each female lays many hundreds of thousands of eggs, which float to the surface and are eaten by fish and other marine predators. Only a tiny number become adults.

Size comparison

Golden perch   Estuary perch   Sooty grunter   Jungle perch   Macquarie perch   Silver perch

PERCH, SAUGER, WALLEYE, & ZANDER

The Percidae is a large and diverse family of fish consisting of perch and related species. These are characterized by their long, slender bodies and their two dorsal fins, separate in some species but joined in others, with the first dorsal having spines and the second having soft rays. The members of the Percidae are found both in streams and in stillwaters. The small species and the young of the large ones feed on insect larvae and other invertebrates; the adults of the large species are fish-eaters.

Perch scales
Perch feel rough to the touch because they have ctenoid scales – scales that have fine teeth on their exposed edges. Smooth scales with no teeth, such as those of the carp family, are called cycloid scales.

Perch eggs
The European perch and the yellow perch both spawn in spring and lay their eggs in long, lacelike ribbons. These are deposited on stones, or woven among water plants and tree roots, in the shallows of still or slow-flowing waters.

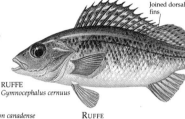

Joined dorsal fins

RUFFE
Gymnocephalus cernuus

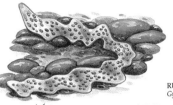

Many dark marks on first dorsal fin

SAUGER
Stizostedion canadense

RUFFE
The diminutive ruffe, or pope, is one of the smallest of the perch family to be of interest to anglers as a quarry. It usually grows to about 6 oz (170 g), but can reach 1 lb 10 oz (750 g).

WALLEYE
Stizostedion vitreum

ZANDER
The zander, or pikeperch, preys heavily on small fish such as bream, ruffe, and roach, and can reach a weight of over 26 lb 8 oz (12 kg). It was originally found in the Danube and other waters of northern and central Europe, but it has been introduced as far west as England and its range is slowly spreading. Some introductions have been controversial, with the zander being blamed for drastic reductions in local fish populations, but in many waters the introductions seem to have caused no major problems.

SAUGER
The genus *Stizostedion* includes the sauger, walleye, and zander, collectively known as pikeperch, which have only slight genetic differences and are very similar in appearance and habits. Like all pikeperch, the sauger is a predator; it can reach a maximum weight of more than 8 lb (3.6 kg).

WALLEYE
The walleye is so named because of its large, glassy eyes, which are distinctive in daylight and glow at night when a light is shone on them, like the eyes of a cat. It is the largest of the North American perches, typically reaching 3 lb (1.36 kg) with a maximum of 25 lb (11.3 kg), and is a prized food fish as well as being a favorite quarry of anglers.

Size comparison

 Zander
 Walleye
 Sauger
 European perch
Volga zander
 Yellow perch
Ruffe

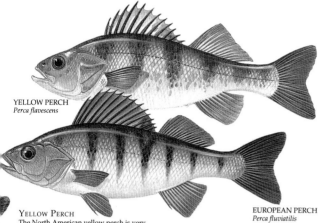

YELLOW PERCH
Perca flavescens

EUROPEAN PERCH
Perca fluviatilis

YELLOW PERCH

The North American yellow perch is very similar to the European perch in appearance and habits, and the two species are closely related. Like all the large members of the Percidae, they make excellent eating and are among the tastiest of freshwater fish.

EUROPEAN PERCH

This perch is widespread in stillwaters and slow-flowing lowland rivers throughout Europe. It is a schooling fish that feeds on insects and small fish, including perch fry, and in some waters of the European mainland it can attain a weight of up to 14 lb (6.5 kg).

DISTRIBUTION

Sauger, walleye: Northwest Territories east to Quebec, southeast to Alabama.
Zander: northern and central Europe; also introduced into western Europe and England.
Volga zander: river systems entering the northern Black and Caspian Seas.
Ruffe: eastern England to Asia; introduced into Scotland and the Great Lakes.
European perch: from Ireland to Siberia; has been introduced into Australia.
Yellow perch: found from the Northwest Territories to the Atlantic drainages as far south as South Carolina.

ZANDER
Stizostedion lucioperca

Eggs

Spawning zander
Zander spawn in spring and early summer, laying clumps of pale yellow eggs on plants or on sand and stones. The larvae hatch after a few days and live on their yolk sacs until their teeth develop and they can feed themselves. Young zander feed on small prey, such as insect larvae and fish fry.

VOLGA ZANDER
Stizostedion volgensis

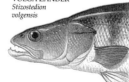

FISHING NOTES

Techniques
Legering, float fishing, and spinning are all effective.

Tackle
For legering and float fishing, try a 10 to 12 ft (3 to 3.7 m) slow or medium-action rod with a spinning reel. Use 5 lb (2.27 kg) mono line and hook sizes 4 to 10 for ruffe and perch, and 6 to 10 lb (2.7 to 4.54 kg) mono with a 20 in (50 cm) wire leader and size 10 treble hook for walleye, sauger, and zander. When spinning, for perch use a 7 to

9 ft (2.1 to 2.7 m) spinning rod with a spinning reel, 5 or 6 lb (2.27 or 2.7 kg) mono line, and a swivelled leader; for walleye, sauger, and zander, use an 8 ft (2.4 m) medium-action spinning rod, spinning reel, 6 to 8 lb (2.7 to 3.6 kg) mono line, and a short, fine-wire leader.

Bait
Worms and maggots for perch, small fish for walleye, sauger, and zander. Spinning: spinners, spoons, jigs, plugs.

VOLGA ZANDER

The appearance of the Volga zander is similar to that of the zander, but the dark markings on its back are much more well defined. It is also generally smaller, and lacks the long fangs of the zander, although its mouth is well equipped with small, sharp teeth. The Volga zander is found in rivers flowing into the Caspian and Black seas, including the Volga itself and the Danube as far upstream as Vienna. It prefers open, deep water to vegetated areas, and grows to about 4 lb 6 oz (2 kg).

CHAR

The most obvious difference between char (salmonids of the genus *Salvelinus*) and salmon and trout (genera *Salmo* and *Oncorhynchus*) lies in their coloration: char have light markings on a darker background; salmon and trout have dark markings on a lighter background. Char feed on invertebrates and small fish, and they are native to the cool waters of the northern parts of the Northern Hemisphere; they are all excellent angling species. Lake and brook trout have been widely introduced elsewhere.

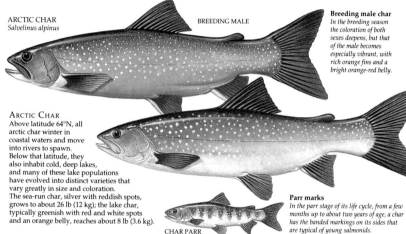

ARCTIC CHAR
Salvelinus alpinus

BREEDING MALE

Breeding male char
In the breeding season the coloration of both sexes deepens, but that of the male becomes especially vibrant, with rich orange fins and a bright orange-red belly.

ARCTIC CHAR
Above latitude 64°N, all arctic char winter in coastal waters and move into rivers to spawn. Below that latitude, they also inhabit cold, deep lakes, and many of these lake populations have evolved into distinct varieties that vary greatly in size and coloration. The sea-run char, silver with reddish spots, grows to about 26 lb (12 kg); the lake char, typically greenish with red and white spots and an orange belly, reaches about 8 lb (3.6 kg).

CHAR PARR

Parr marks
In the parr stage of its life cycle, from a few months up to about two years of age, a char has the banded markings on its sides that are typical of young salmonids.

Hybrids
Hybridization among members of the Salmonidae family occurs both naturally and as a result of selective breeding by fish farms. Natural hybrids include Atlantic salmon × sea trout and rainbow × cutthroat; farmed crossbreeds include the splake (brook trout × lake trout), the tiger trout (brook × brown), and the cheetah trout (brook × rainbow).

SPLAKE (HYBRID)

FISHING NOTES

Techniques
Fly fishing, spinning and trolling for arctic char and lake trout; fly fishing and spinning for brook trout and Dolly Varden.

Tackle
For fly fishing use a 8 to 11 ft (2.4 to 3.4 m) fly rod with a fly reel, floating or sinking line as appropriate, and flies dressed on hook sizes 10 to 14. For spinning and for shallow trolling try a 9 ft (2.7 m), medium spinning rod with a spinning reel, and use 4 to 6 lb (1.8 to 2.7 kg) line for spinning and 10 to 15 lb (4.54 to 6.8 kg) line for shallow trolling work.

For deep trolling, use a 6ft (1.8m), fast-taper trolling rod with braided wire line; the rod should have hardened rings or roller guides to resist the abrasive action of the wire line.

Bait
For arctic char, use small, bright spinners or spoons, or wet-fly patterns that incorporate a flashy material such as gold or silver tinsel, for example Butcher or Mallard and Claret. Use large, trolled spoons or livebait for lake trout in deep water, and spoons, spinners, plugs, or streamer flies when the fish are close inshore. Brook trout and Dolly Varden may be taken on lures, dry flies, wet flies, and nymphs.

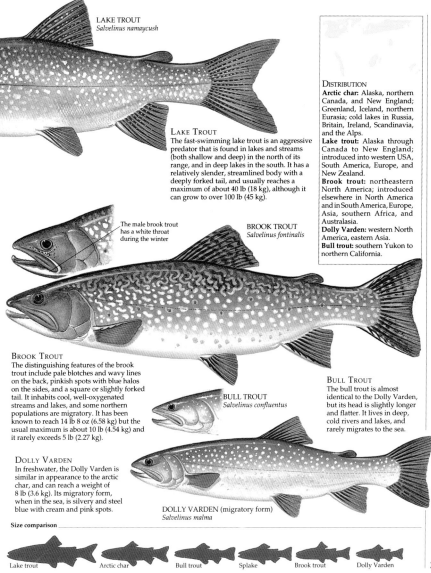

LAKE TROUT
Salvelinus namaycush

LAKE TROUT
The fast-swimming lake trout is an aggressive predator that is found in lakes and streams (both shallow and deep) in the north of its range, and in deep lakes in the south. It has a relatively slender, streamlined body with a deeply forked tail, and usually reaches a maximum of about 40 lb (18 kg), although it can grow to over 100 lb (45 kg).

The male brook trout has a white throat during the winter

BROOK TROUT
Salvelinus fontinalis

DISTRIBUTION
Arctic char: Alaska, northern Canada, and New England; Greenland, Iceland, northern Eurasia; cold lakes in Russia, Britain, Ireland, Scandinavia, and the Alps.
Lake trout: Alaska through Canada to New England; introduced into western USA, South America, Europe, and New Zealand.
Brook trout: northeastern North America; introduced elsewhere in North America and in South America, Europe, Asia, southern Africa, and Australasia.
Dolly Varden: western North America, eastern Asia.
Bull trout: southern Yukon to northern California.

BROOK TROUT
The distinguishing features of the brook trout include pale blotches and wavy lines on the back, pinkish spots with blue halos on the sides, and a square or slightly forked tail. It inhabits cool, well-oxygenated streams and lakes, and some northern populations are migratory. It has been known to reach 14 lb 8 oz (6.58 kg) but the usual maximum is about 10 lb (4.54 kg) and it rarely exceeds 5 lb (2.27 kg).

BULL TROUT
Salvelinus confluentus

BULL TROUT
The bull trout is almost identical to the Dolly Varden, but its head is slightly longer and flatter. It lives in deep, cold rivers and lakes, and rarely migrates to the sea.

DOLLY VARDEN
In freshwater, the Dolly Varden is similar in appearance to the arctic char, and can reach a weight of 8 lb (3.6 kg). Its migratory form, when in the sea, is silvery and steel blue with cream and pink spots.

DOLLY VARDEN (migratory form)
Salvelinus malma

Size comparison

Lake trout · Arctic char · Bull trout · Splake · Brook trout · Dolly Varden

Freshwater SPECIES

SALMON

Salmon are some of the most important commercial and sport fish in the world. All begin their lives in freshwater and most migrate to the sea to mature, returning to freshwater to spawn. The principal exceptions are the landlocked varieties of the Atlantic and sockeye salmon, and two Eurasian landlocked species, the huchen (*Hucho hucho*) and the taimen (*Hucho taimen*). The huchen, a fish of the Danube basin, is now a protected species in many of its native waters but has been introduced successfully into some French rivers; the taimen is common in the Volga basin and Siberia.

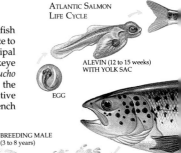

ATLANTIC SALMON
LIFE CYCLE

ALEVIN (12 to 15 weeks)
WITH YOLK SAC

EGG

Life cycles
The life cycles of all the salmon species are broadly similar. The main differences are that the Pacific species die after spawning but many Atlantic salmon spawn more than once; the landlocked species do not migrate to the sea but mature in freshwater; and there are some differences in timing. The eggs are laid in redds (nests) scooped out of gravel by the female, and take from 70 to 200 days to hatch.

BREEDING MALE
(3 to 8 years)

ATLANTIC SALMON
Salmo salar

COHO SALMON
Oncorhynchus kisutch

BREEDING
MALE

Spots on
upper lobe
only

Coloration
The coloration of a salmon changes when it is ready to breed, and the male develops a hook (kype) on its lower jaw.

BREEDING
MALE CHINOOK

COHO SALMON
The coho or silver salmon is an important sport fish both in its native waters and those to which it has been introduced, such as the Great Lakes. It is similar to the chinook, but has white gums rather than black, less extensive spotting on the tail, and is smaller, reaching a maximum of around 33 lb (15 kg).

MASU SALMON
The relatively small and stocky masu, or cherry salmon, is an Asian species with both migratory and freshwater forms. It reaches maturity in three or four years, growing to about 10 lb (4.54 kg), and is fished for commercially as well as for sport.

MASU SALMON
Oncorhynchus masou

PINK SALMON
Oncorhynchus gorbuscha

BREEDING
MALE PINK

FISHING NOTES

Techniques
The Atlantic salmon is fished for in freshwater. The most usual technique is fly fishing, but it is also taken on spoons, plugs, and natural baits on waters (and at times of the year) where these methods are permitted. Pacific salmon, of which the chinook and coho are the most important species for the sport fisherman, are usually taken by trolling just offshore and in estuaries, but they are also caught by fly fishing and spinning (as are the landlocked varieties) when they move into freshwater to spawn.

Tackle
Fly tackle for freshwater salmon fishing is typically a 12 to 16 ft (3.7 to 4.9 m) rod, a fly reel, and weight-forward fly line. For spinning and bait fishing, try a heavy 10 ft (3 m) spinning rod with a baitcaster reel and 15 to 20 lb (6.8 to 9.1 kg) line. The usual saltwater rig for chinook and coho is a boat or trolling rod with a star-drag baitcaster reel and 20 to 45 lb (9.1 to 20.4 kg) line.

Bait
In freshwater, use flies, lures, worms, or prawns. In saltwater, use streamers, lures, or fish baits.

PINK SALMON
Because of the distinctively humped back of the spawning male, the pink salmon is also known as the humpback or humpy. It is the most abundant of the Pacific species and is of considerable commercial importance, but it is a small fish, usually averaging 3 to 5 lb (1.36 to 2.27 kg) with a maximum of 12 lb (5.4 kg).

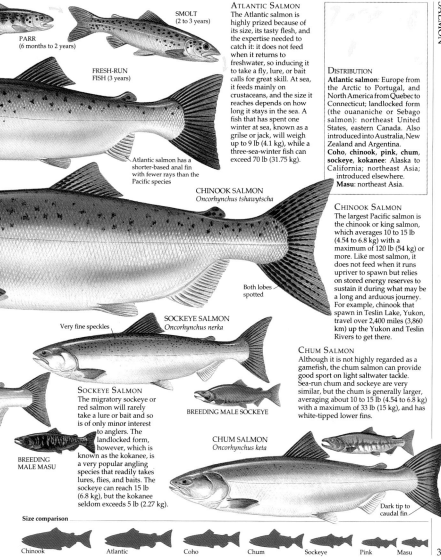

PARR
(6 months to 2 years)

SMOLT
(2 to 3 years)

FRESH-RUN
FISH (3 years)

ATLANTIC SALMON

The Atlantic salmon is highly prized because of its size, its tasty flesh, and the expertise needed to catch it: it does not feed when it returns to freshwater, so inducing it to take a fly, lure, or bait calls for great skill. At sea, it feeds mainly on crustaceans, and the size it reaches depends on how long it stays in the sea. A fish that has spent one winter at sea, known as a grilse or jack, will weigh up to 9 lb (4.1 kg), while a three-sea-winter fish can exceed 70 lb (31.75 kg).

Atlantic salmon has a shorter-based anal fin with fewer rays than the Pacific species

DISTRIBUTION
Atlantic salmon: Europe from the Arctic to Portugal, and North America from Quebec to Connecticut; landlocked form (the ouananiche or Sebago salmon): northeast United States, eastern Canada. Also introduced into Australia, New Zealand and Argentina.
Coho, **chinook**, **pink**, **chum**, **sockeye**, **kokanee**: Alaska to California; northeast Asia; introduced elsewhere.
Masu: northeast Asia.

CHINOOK SALMON
Oncorhynchus tshawytscha

Both lobes spotted

CHINOOK SALMON
The largest Pacific salmon is the chinook or king salmon, which averages 10 to 15 lb (4.54 to 6.8 kg) with a maximum of 120 lb (54 kg) or more. Like most salmon, it does not feed when it runs upriver to spawn but relies on stored energy reserves to sustain it during what may be a long and arduous journey. For example, chinook that spawn in Teslin Lake, Yukon, travel over 2,400 miles (3,860 km) up the Yukon and Teslin Rivers to get there.

CHUM SALMON
Although it is not highly regarded as a gamefish, the chum salmon can provide good sport on light saltwater tackle. Sea-run chum and sockeye are very similar, but the chum is generally larger, averaging about 10 to 15 lb (4.54 to 6.8 kg) with a maximum of 33 lb (15 kg), and has white-tipped lower fins.

Very fine speckles

SOCKEYE SALMON
Oncorhynchus nerka

SOCKEYE SALMON
The migratory sockeye or red salmon will rarely take a lure or bait and so is of only minor interest to anglers. The landlocked form, however, which is known as the kokanee, is a very popular angling species that readily takes lures, flies, and baits. The sockeye can reach 15 lb (6.8 kg), but the kokanee seldom exceeds 5 lb (2.27 kg).

BREEDING MALE SOCKEYE

BREEDING MALE MASU

CHUM SALMON
Oncorhynchus keta

Dark tip to caudal fin

Size comparison

Chinook   Atlantic   Coho   Chum   Sockeye   Pink   Masu

37

Freshwater SPECIES

TROUT

The brown trout and the rainbow trout are two of the world's most important gamefish species, and because of the high-quality sport they offer their distribution has been increased by extensive introduction programs. The cutthroat trout, despite its qualities as a gamefish, has not been widely introduced beyond its natural range for a number of reasons, such as its tendency to hybridize with the rainbow trout. Trout thrive in cool, clean streams and lakes and feed mainly on insects, insect larvae, crustaceans, and fish. When at sea, the migratory forms eat fish and crustaceans.

RAINBOW TROUT

The rainbow trout varies greatly in appearance and size, and there are many different races and subspecies such as the Kamloops, Shasta, and Kern River rainbows. Most, however, have a pink stripe along the lateral line and small black speckles on the sides, back, upper fins, and tail. In North America, rainbows weighing more than 50 lb (22.7 kg) have been recorded, but the usual maximum in European waters is only around 24 lb (11 kg).

STEELHEAD

Steelhead are rainbow trout that migrate to sea before returning to rivers to spawn, or live in lakes and move into streams to spawn. Fresh-run steelhead are silvery, but their coloration soon changes to resemble that of non-migratory rainbows.

SEA TROUT
Migratory form of brown trout

Sharply squared-off tail

BROWN TROUT
Salmo trutta

SEA TROUT

The sea trout, the silvery migratory form of the brown trout, enters the sea at about two years old but returns to rivers to spawn. A large sea trout resembles an Atlantic salmon (*see page 36*), but its tail has a thicker "wrist" and is more squared-off.

BROWN TROUT

The brown trout is highly variable in appearance and size, and these variations are caused by environmental and genetic factors. In general, the body is brownish and sprinkled with black and red spots, and its weight ranges from under 1 lb (454 g) in small streams to over 30 lb (13.6 kg) in large waters.

FISHING NOTES

Techniques
Trout are taken on natural baits and on spinners, but fly fishing is without any doubt the preeminent trout-fishing technique.

Tackle
For fly fishing, use a 6 to 11 ft (1.8 to 3.4 m) fly rod, a fly reel, and floating or sinking line as appropriate. To fish for trout with naturals, such as worms, use a 7 to 10 ft (2.1 to 3 m) medium-action rod with a

spinning reel, 4 to 8 lb (1.8 to 3.6 kg) line, and hook sizes 6 to 14. For spinning with artificial lures, try a 7 to 9 ft (2.1 to 2.7 m) spinning rod with a spinning reel and 4 to 8 lb (1.8 to 3.6 kg) line.

Bait
For fly fishing, use whichever pattern is appropriate for the water, the style of fishing, and the prevailing conditions. For spinning, use small spinners, spoons, and plugs. Suitable naturals for trout include larvae and worms.

Hooked jaw

Cannibal trout
Although all brown trout are carnivorous, large individuals will even eat smaller members of their own species. These cannibal trout, which develop a distinctly hooked lower jaw, lurk in deep water waiting to pounce on their prey as it swims past.

38

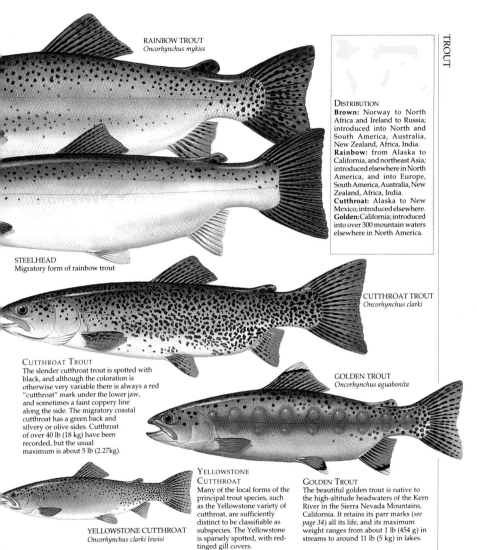

RAINBOW TROUT
Oncorhynchus mykiss

STEELHEAD
Migratory form of rainbow trout

DISTRIBUTION
Brown: Norway to North Africa and Ireland to Russia; introduced into North and South America, Australia, New Zealand, Africa, India.
Rainbow: from Alaska to California, and northeast Asia; introduced elsewhere in North America, and into Europe, South America, Australia, New Zealand, Africa, India.
Cutthroat: Alaska to New Mexico; introduced elsewhere.
Golden: California; introduced into over 300 mountain waters elsewhere in North America.

CUTTHROAT TROUT
Oncorhynchus clarki

GOLDEN TROUT
Oncorhynchus aguabonita

CUTTHROAT TROUT
The slender cutthroat trout is spotted with black, and although the coloration is otherwise very variable there is always a red "cutthroat" mark under the lower jaw, and sometimes a faint coppery line along the side. The migratory coastal cutthroat has a green back and silvery or olive sides. Cutthroat of over 40 lb (18 kg) have been recorded, but the usual maximum is about 5 lb (2.27kg).

YELLOWSTONE CUTTHROAT
Many of the local forms of the principal trout species, such as the Yellowstone variety of cutthroat, are sufficiently distinct to be classifiable as subspecies. The Yellowstone is sparsely spotted, with red-tinged gill covers.

GOLDEN TROUT
The beautiful golden trout is native to the high-altitude headwaters of the Kern River in the Sierra Nevada Mountains, California. It retains its parr marks (*see page 34*) all its life, and its maximum weight ranges from about 1 lb (454 g) in streams to around 11 lb (5 kg) in lakes.

YELLOWSTONE CUTTHROAT
Oncorhynchus clarki lewisi

Size comparison

Sea trout   Steelhead   Cutthroat trout   Rainbow trout   Golden trout   Stream brown trout

39

WHITEFISH & GRAYLING

Whitefish and grayling are widely distributed in the colder lakes and streams of the Northern Hemisphere. Grayling are popular angling species, as are several of the whitefish, but many whitefish species are threatened with extinction and it is illegal to fish for them in many countries and on certain waters. Grayling feed mainly on bottom-dwelling creatures such as insect larvae, crustaceans, and worms, but will also take insects at the surface. The whitefish's diet ranges from plankton to fish.

INCONNU

The large, powerful inconnu, or sheefish, is the only predatory whitefish in North America. Its average weight is about 5 lb (2.27 kg), but it can live for over 20 years and has been known to reach weights of up to 55 lb (25 kg). Most inconnu live in the estuaries and lower reaches of rivers and migrate upstream to spawn, but there are some non-migratory lake populations. The young fish feed on plankton at first, and then on small, bottom-dwelling creatures before becoming predatory during their second year.

INCONNU
Stenodus leucichthys

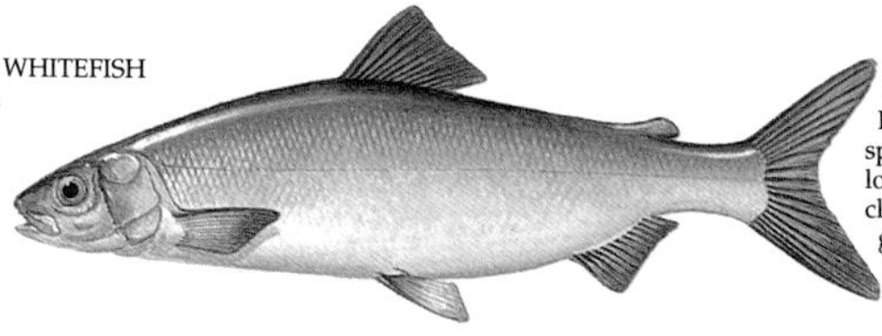

Protruding
lower jaw

EUROPEAN WHITEFISH
Coregonus sp.

EUROPEAN WHITEFISH

In Europe, the many whitefish species, subspecies, races, and local variants have yet to be classified definitively. In general, they are at best of minor interest to anglers, but many are netted commercially because of their tasty flesh. Common names include vendace, houting, powan, and schelly; they are slender, silvery fish that range in size from about 1 lb (454 g) (*Coregonus albula*) to around 11 lb (5 kg) (*C. pallasi*).

CISCO

Because of its herringlike size, shape, and general appearance, the cisco is also known as the lake herring. Despite being a small fish, rarely exceeding 2 lb (910 g), it is popular with anglers because it will readily take a wide range of lures and baits, including flies.

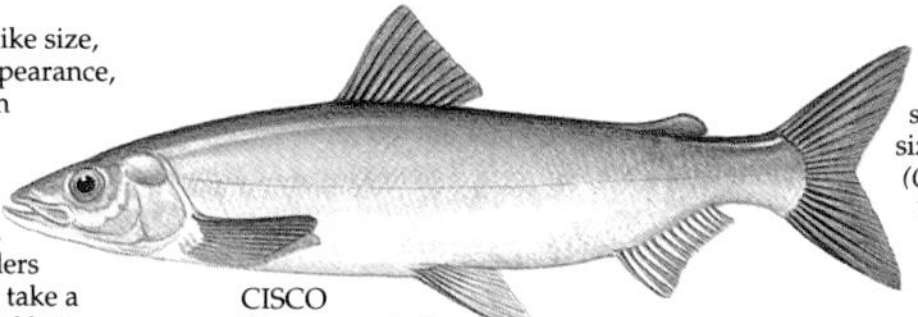

CISCO
Coregonus artedi

Size comparison

Inconnu

Lake whitefish

Grayling

Cisco

European whitefish

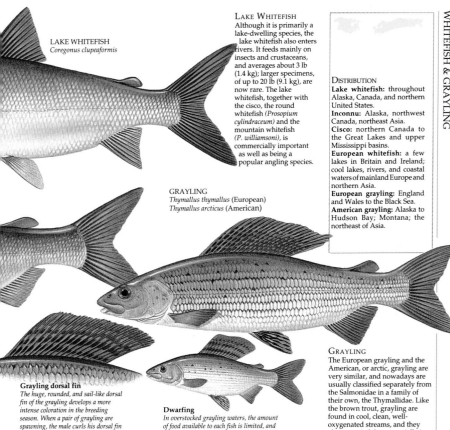

LAKE WHITEFISH
Coregonus clupeaformis

LAKE WHITEFISH
Although it is primarily a lake-dwelling species, the lake whitefish also enters rivers. It feeds mainly on insects and crustaceans, and averages about 3 lb (1.4 kg); larger specimens, of up to 20 lb (9.1 kg), are now rare. The lake whitefish, together with the cisco, the round whitefish (*Prosopium cylindraceum*) and the mountain whitefish (*P. williamsoni*), is commercially important as well as being a popular angling species.

DISTRIBUTION
Lake whitefish: throughout Alaska, Canada, and northern United States.
Inconnu: Alaska, northwest Canada, northeast Asia.
Cisco: northern Canada to the Great Lakes and upper Mississippi basins.
European whitefish: a few lakes in Britain and Ireland; cool lakes, rivers, and coastal waters of mainland Europe and northern Asia.
European grayling: England and Wales to the Black Sea.
American grayling: Alaska to Hudson Bay; Montana; the northeast of Asia.

GRAYLING
Thymallus thymallus (European)
Thymallus arcticus (American)

Grayling dorsal fin
The huge, rounded, and sail-like dorsal fin of the grayling develops a more intense coloration in the breeding season. When a pair of grayling are spawning, the male curls his dorsal fin over the female.

Dwarfing
In overstocked grayling waters, the amount of food available to each fish is limited, and small, deep-bodied individuals are common.

GRAYLING
The European grayling and the American, or arctic, grayling are very similar, and nowadays are usually classified separately from the Salmonidae in a family of their own, the Thymallidae. Like the brown trout, grayling are found in cool, clean, well-oxygenated streams, and they also occur in lakes, especially in North America. Grayling are relatively small, with a maximum weight of about 6 lb (2.7 kg).

FISHING NOTES

Techniques
Whitefish and grayling are taken by fly fishing, by spinning with artificial baits, and also by float fishing or legering with natural baits.

Tackle
For fly fishing, try an 8 to 9 ft (2.4 to 2.7 m) medium-action fly rod with a fly reel and #5 to #7 line. For float fishing or legering, try a 11 to 13 ft (3.4 to 4 m) rod with a spinning reel, 2 to 3 lb (910 g to 1.36 kg) line, and hook sizes 10 to 16. For spinning, use an ultralight rod for grayling and cisco, and a medium-action rod for inconnu and lake whitefish.

Bait
Use imitative dry flies, wet flies, and nymphs for grayling, streamers for inconnu, and dry flies for cisco and lake whitefish. When spinning, use small, bright spinners and spoons. Natural baits for grayling include maggots and small worms; lake whitefish can be taken on cut fish.

Breeding grayling
Grayling spawn in gravelly shallows in spring and early summer, lake fish entering streams to spawn. The hatchlings lurk among stones, living off their yolk sacs.

BONEFISH, BLUEFISH, & TARPON

Saltwater SPECIES

These fish haunt the shallow coastal waters of the tropical and warm-temperate regions of the world, and are among the most exciting and popular marine sports species. The food of bonefish (the Albulidae) and tarpon (the Elopidae) consists mainly of crustaceans and small fish, but the bluefish (a member of the Pomatomidae) is a savage predator that will eat virtually anything edible that crosses its path.

BONEFISH

The bonefish is a bottom feeder that grubs in the mud or sand for food such as shrimps and crabs. In very shallow water, the tails of feeding bonefish often break the surface, betraying their presence to stalking anglers who wade the mudflats in pursuit of them. Adult bonefish typically weigh up to 10 lb (4.54 kg) but can reach 19 lb (8.6 kg).

Vertical bars fade with age

BONEFISH
Albula vulpes

TARPON
Megalops atlanticus

BLUEFISH
Pomatomus saltatrix

BLUEFISH

The highly migratory bluefish can grow to over 50 lb (23 kg), and travels in huge schools that go into a feeding frenzy when they encounter schools of prey fish such as herring or menhaden. They have been known to come close inshore and attack bathers, and their sharp, prominent, triangular teeth can inflict painful wounds. They should be handled with care when caught, especially when they are being unhooked.

TARPON

The large, silvery tarpon is usually caught in tidal creeks, estuaries, mangrove swamps, and lagoons, and can sometimes be taken offshore. Its scales are large and tough, with a bright, metallic sheen, and the last ray of the dorsal fin is greatly elongated. Most tarpon landed by anglers weigh between 20 and 80 lb (9.1 and 36.3 kg), but the maximum weight is much higher and individuals of over 300 lb (136 kg) have been reported.

FISHING NOTES

Techniques
The usual techniques are trolling for bluefish, and spinning and fly fishing for bonefish and tarpon.

Tackle
For bluefish, use a 20 lb (9.1 kg) class boat rod with a 4/0 baitcaster, 20 lb (9.1 kg) nylon or Dacron line, a trolling weight, a wire terminal leader, and hook sizes 4/0 to 6/0. When spinning for bonefish and tarpon, try a 6½ to 7 ft (2 to 2.1 m) medium-action rod and spinning reel. Use 8 lb (3.6 kg) mono line with a mono leader for bonefish, and 15 lb (6.8 kg) mono line with

a short wire leader for tarpon. Suitable fly tackle for bonefish and tarpon would be a 9 to 10 ft (2.7 to 3 m) saltwater fly rod and a 4 in (10 cm) reel, with 8 lb (3.6 kg) backing for bonefish and 27 lb (12.2 kg) backing for tarpon; hook sizes are 6 to 1/0 for bonefish, 2 to 5/0 for tarpon.

Bait
Bluefish are usually taken on plugs or baitfish. For bonefish, spin with small leadhead lures and use shrimp imitator patterns, bucktails, and small imitation marabou streamers for fly fishing. For tarpon, spin with medium-sized plugs, and use yellow or orange splayed-wing streamers for fly fishing.

Hard fighter
The hard-fighting tarpon is justifiably regarded as one of the world's most exciting gamefish. As soon as it feels the hook being set, it begins a series of spectacular, twisting leaps in an effort to free itself, and it very often succeeds in doing so.

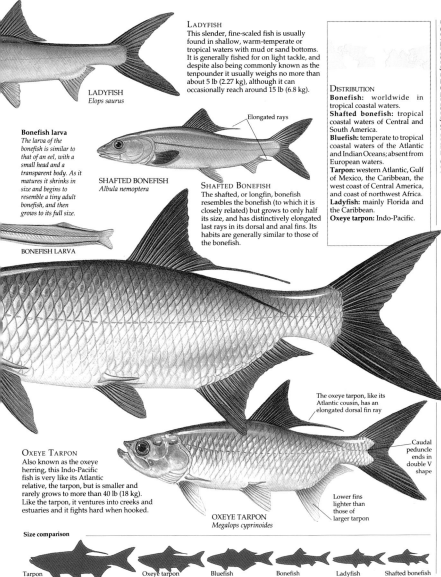

LADYFISH

This slender, fine-scaled fish is usually found in shallow, warm-temperate or tropical waters with mud or sand bottoms. It is generally fished for on light tackle, and despite also being commonly known as the tenpounder it usually weighs no more than about 5 lb (2.27 kg), although it can occasionally reach around 15 lb (6.8 kg).

LADYFISH
Elops saurus

Bonefish larva
The larva of the bonefish is similar to that of an eel, with a small head and a transparent body. As it matures it shrinks in size and begins to resemble a tiny adult bonefish, and then grows to its full size.

BONEFISH LARVA

Elongated rays

SHAFTED BONEFISH
Albula nemoptera

SHAFTED BONEFISH

The shafted, or longfin, bonefish resembles the bonefish (to which it is closely related) but grows to only half its size, and has distinctively elongated last rays in its dorsal and anal fins. Its habits are generally similar to those of the bonefish.

DISTRIBUTION

Bonefish: worldwide in tropical coastal waters.
Shafted bonefish: tropical coastal waters of Central and South America.
Bluefish: temperate to tropical coastal waters of the Atlantic and Indian Oceans; absent from European waters.
Tarpon: western Atlantic, Gulf of Mexico, the Caribbean, the west coast of Central America, and coast of northwest Africa.
Ladyfish: mainly Florida and the Caribbean.
Oxeye tarpon: Indo-Pacific.

The oxeye tarpon, like its Atlantic cousin, has an elongated dorsal fin ray

Caudal peduncle ends in double V shape

OXEYE TARPON

Also known as the oxeye herring, this Indo-Pacific fish is very like its Atlantic relative, the tarpon, but is smaller and rarely grows to more than 40 lb (18 kg). Like the tarpon, it ventures into creeks and estuaries and it fights hard when hooked.

OXEYE TARPON
Megalops cyprinoides

Lower fins lighter than those of larger tarpon

Size comparison

Tarpon   Oxeye tarpon   Bluefish   Bonefish   Ladyfish   Shafted bonefish

43

EELS

Saltwater SPECIES

There are more than 20 families of eel, including the Muraenidae (morays) and Congridae (congers), and all but one of them consist of exclusively saltwater fish. The exception is the family Anguillidae, which includes the American, European, and longfinned eels, all of which mature in freshwater and travel to the sea to spawn. The American and European eels travel to the Sargasso Sea, an area in the North Atlantic; the longfinned eel and the other Australasian species of Anguillidae migrate to the Indian Ocean.

CONGER
Conger conger

MORAY

The European moray *Muraena helena*, found in the eastern Atlantic and the Mediterranean, is one of the more than 80 species of moray. All are notoriously short-tempered and quick to use their razor-sharp teeth when they feel threatened. They are rarely fished for, but are sometimes hooked when other species are being sought. *M. helena* can reach 4 ft 3 in (1.3 m) but is usually much smaller.

MORAY
Muraena helena

CALIFORNIA MORAY

This moray is found in shallow water along the coasts of California and Baja California, from Point Conception south. It attains a maximum length of about 5 ft (1.5 m).

CALIFORNIA MORAY
Gymnothorax mordax

AMERICAN EEL
Anguilla rostrata

AMERICAN EEL

Adult American eels usually spend several years in freshwater, the males staying near the mouths of rivers and the females traveling far upstream. The females grow to 3 ft 3 in (1 m) or more and a weight of over 11 lb (5 kg), but the males are much smaller, generally around 1 ft (30 cm) in length.

EUROPEAN EEL
Anguilla anguilla

EUROPEAN EEL

The European eel is very similar to its American counterpart, and the two may be a single species. After spawning, the adults die; the journey to freshwater takes young American eels about a year, and young European eels three or four years.

LONG-FINNED EEL
Anguilla reinhardtii

LONGFINNED EEL

This is one of a number of freshwater eels found in Australasia. Like the American and European eels, it migrates to the sea to spawn, possibly in the Coral Sea. It grows to 31 lb (14 kg).

Eel larvae
In the early stages of their development, eel larvae are strange, transparent, leaflike creatures called leptocephali. Later, they become elvers, miniature versions of their parents, and it is as elvers that freshwater eels arrive in rivers.

EARLY STAGE

LATER STAGE

Size comparison

| Conger   California moray   Moray   Longfinned eel   American eel   European eel

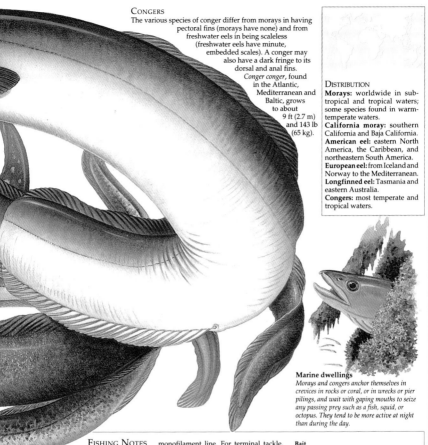

CONGERS

The various species of conger differ from morays in having pectoral fins (morays have none) and from freshwater eels in being scaleless (freshwater eels have minute, embedded scales). A conger may also have a dark fringe to its dorsal and anal fins.

Conger conger, found in the Atlantic, Mediterranean and Baltic, grows to about 9 ft (2.7 m) and 143 lb (65 kg).

DISTRIBUTION

Morays: worldwide in subtropical and tropical waters; some species found in warm-temperate waters.
California moray: southern California and Baja California.
American eel: eastern North America, the Caribbean, and northeastern South America.
European eel: from Iceland and Norway to the Mediterranean.
Longfinned eel: Tasmania and eastern Australia.
Congers: most temperate and tropical waters.

Marine dwellings
Morays and congers anchor themselves in crevices in rocks or coral, or in wrecks or pier pilings, and wait with gaping mouths to seize any passing prey such as a fish, squid, or octopus. They tend to be more active at night than during the day.

FISHING NOTES

Techniques
The migratory eels are usually fished for in freshwater, by legering. Marine eels (conger and moray) are taken by fishing with natural baits from rocky shores, piers, jetties, and sea walls, and from boats over rocks and wrecks.

Tackle
For migratory eels, use a 10 to 12 ft (3 to 3.7 m), 2 lb (910 g) test curve, carp or pike rod, with a spinning reel, and 5 lb (2.27 kg) monofilament line. For terminal tackle, use a running leger or fish the bait freelined, with a size 4 to 8 hook tied direct to the line. When fishing from the shore for marine eels, use a 20 to 50 lb (9.1 to 22.7 kg) class surfcasting rod, a 4/0 baitcaster reel, 30 to 35 lb (13.6 to 15.9 kg) line, a running leger wire leader, a pear- or pyramid-shaped weight, and a 6/0 hook. To fish from a boat for marine eels, try a 50 lb (22.7 kg) boat rod, 8/0 baitcaster reel, and 50 to 60 lb (22.7 to 27.2 kg) line. Use a wire leader, a size 8/0 hook, and a pear- or pyramid-shaped weight.

Bait
Worms are good bait for freshwater eels, as are small, dead fish. Fish baits are very effective for large eels, and they should be whole, about 5 in (13 cm) long, and punctured so that they sink. Pungent baits such as fish liver and smoked fish are also effective, and it is worth using an oily, smelly, non-floating groundbait to attract eels into the swim you are going to fish.

The marine eels can be caught on large natural baits, such as whole or cut fish, squid, and cuttlefish, and these baits should be fished on the bottom.

ARIIDAE; SPHYRAENIDAE

SEA CATFISH & BARRACUDA

The Ariidae family of sea catfish consists of about 80 species, widely distributed around the world in warm coastal waters and estuaries, and also (in the tropics) in freshwater. When caught, a sea catfish must be handled carefully, because the dorsal and pectoral fins have sharp spines that can inflict painful wounds. Barracuda belong to the Sphyraenidae family, which contains about 20 species. They are all fierce predators that feed voraciously on small, schooling species, and because they are attracted to their quarry by sight rather than smell they tend to concentrate on bright, silvery colored prey.

Mouth brooding
In most species of sea catfish, the male keeps the marble-sized fertilized eggs in his mouth until they hatch, which can take up to a month.

HARDHEAD CATFISH
The hardhead catfish, also called the sea catfish, is common in coastal and brackish waters from Massachusetts to Mexico. It has four barbels on its chin and two on its upper jaw, and can reach a weight of 12 lb (5.4 kg) although it usually does not exceed 2 lb (910 g). Several related species are found in the coastal waters, rivers, and lakes of northern Australia, including the blue catfish or salmon catfish (*Arius graeffei*).

HARDHEAD CATFISH
Arius felis

GUAGUANCHE
Like other barracuda, the guaguanche has a slender, cigar-shaped body, two widely separated dorsal fins, and a protruding lower jaw; it is identifiable by the yellow stripe along its lateral line. It is found on both sides of the Atlantic, and grows to a length of about 2 ft (60 cm).

GUAGUANCHE
Sphyraena guachancho

NORTHERN SENNET
Sphyraena borealis

SENNETS
The northern sennet and southern sennet are almost identical, and may in fact be a single species. These little barracuda have the same overall coloration and both grow to about 18 in (45 cm), but the southern sennet has fewer scales on its lateral line (107 to 116 as opposed to 118 to 135) and its eyes are larger. The northern sennet is found from New England to Florida and the Gulf of Mexico, and the southern sennet from Florida to Uruguay. In the eastern Atlantic and the Mediterranean, barracuda are represented by the European barracuda (*Sphyraena sphyraena*).

GREAT BARRACUDA
Sphyraena barracuda

Large eye

SOUTHERN SENNET
Sphyraena picudilla

PACIFIC BARRACUDA
Sphyraena argentea

FISHING NOTES

Techniques
Catfish are caught by bottom fishing from the shore or piers. For barracuda fishing try trolling, or spinning from a boat or from the shore.

Tackle
For catfish, try an 11 or 12 ft (3.4 or 3.7 m) medium-action rod, with a spinning reel, 7 to 15 lb (3.2 to 6.8 kg) mono line, size 4 to 6/0 hook, and a 1 oz (28 g) weight. To troll for barracuda, use a 12 to 30 lb (5.4 to 13.6 kg) class boat rod with a baitcaster reel, 12 to 30 lb (5.4 to 13.6 kg) nylon line with a wire leader, a size 4/0 to 8/0 hook, and a banana-shaped trolling weight. Spinning calls for a medium spinning rod with a spinning reel, 12 to 30 lb (5.4 to 13.6 kg) nylon line with a wire leader, and hook sizes 4/0 to 8/0.

Bait
Cut fish and livebaits such as sandworms are ideal for catfish, which can also be taken on jigs and plugs. For barracuda, use bright, flashy spinners, wooden plugs, strips of fish, and whole fish such as sardines, anchovies, and queenfish.

Barracuda in shallows
Barracuda are often found in shallow water, where their natural curiosity leads them to follow (and sometimes attack) swimmers.

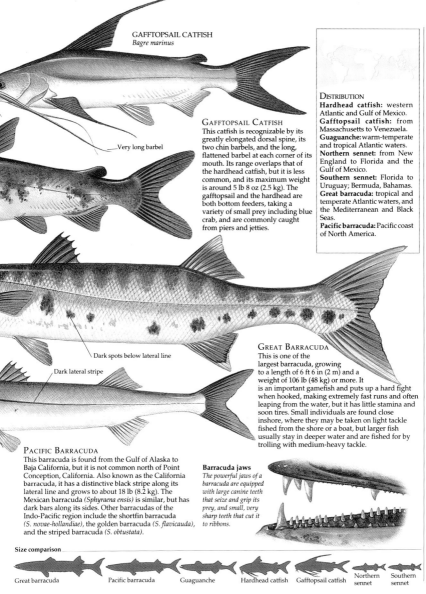

GAFFTOPSAIL CATFISH
Bagre marinus

Very long barbel

GAFFTOPSAIL CATFISH
This catfish is recognizable by its greatly elongated dorsal spine, its two chin barbels, and the long, flattened barbel at each corner of its mouth. Its range overlaps that of the hardhead catfish, but it is less common, and its maximum weight is around 5 lb 8 oz (2.5 kg). The gafftopsail and the hardhead are both bottom feeders, taking a variety of small prey including blue crab, and are commonly caught from piers and jetties.

DISTRIBUTION
Hardhead catfish: western Atlantic and Gulf of Mexico.
Gafftopsail catfish: from Massachusetts to Venezuela.
Guaguanche: warm-temperate and tropical Atlantic waters.
Northern sennet: from New England to Florida and the Gulf of Mexico.
Southern sennet: Florida to Uruguay; Bermuda, Bahamas.
Great barracuda: tropical and temperate Atlantic waters, and the Mediterranean and Black Seas.
Pacific barracuda: Pacific coast of North America.

Dark spots below lateral line

Dark lateral stripe

GREAT BARRACUDA
This is one of the largest barracuda, growing to a length of 6 ft 6 in (2 m) and a weight of 106 lb (48 kg) or more. It is an important gamefish and puts up a hard fight when hooked, making extremely fast runs and often leaping from the water, but it has little stamina and soon tires. Small individuals are found close inshore, where they may be taken on light tackle fished from the shore or a boat, but larger fish usually stay in deeper water and are fished for by trolling with medium-heavy tackle.

PACIFIC BARRACUDA
This barracuda is found from the Gulf of Alaska to Baja California, but it is not common north of Point Conception, California. Also known as the California barracuda, it has a distinctive black stripe along its lateral line and grows to about 18 lb (8.2 kg). The Mexican barracuda (*Sphyraena ensis*) is similar, but has dark bars along its sides. Other barracudas of the Indo-Pacific region include the shortfin barracuda (*S. novae-hollandiae*), the golden barracuda (*S. flavicauda*), and the striped barracuda (*S. obtustata*).

Barracuda jaws
The powerful jaws of a barracuda are equipped with large canine teeth that seize and grip its prey, and small, very sharp teeth that cut it to ribbons.

Size comparison

Great barracuda — Pacific barracuda — Guaguanche — Hardhead catfish — Gafftopsail catfish — Northern sennet — Southern sennet

Saltwater SPECIES

AMBERJACK & JACK

The Carangidae is a large family of predatory marine fish, and has over 200 members including amberjack, jack, and pompano (*see page 50*). They have streamlined bodies with deeply forked tails, the spiny and soft parts of their dorsal fins are separate, and they feed on fish and invertebrates such as squid. Their flesh is tasty, but you should seek local advice before eating any you catch because they can be a source of ciguatera, a distressing type of food poisoning that can be fatal.

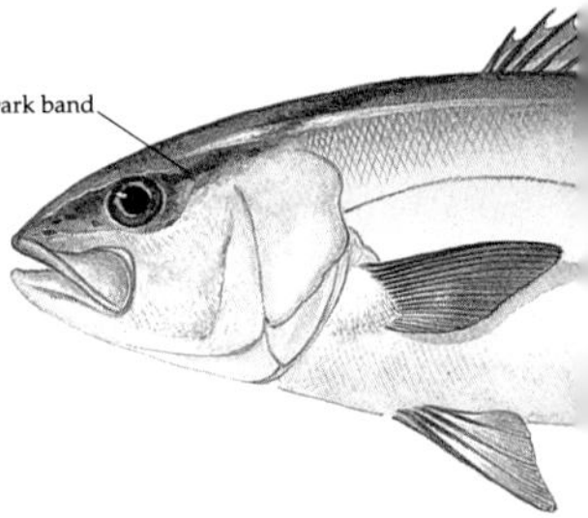

Dark band

ALMACO JACK

The almaco jack is distributed worldwide in warm waters and grows to a weight of 126 lb (57 kg) or more. It is similar to the greater amberjack and the yellowtail, but the dark bands through its eyes are more pronounced, and the front lobe of its soft dorsal fin is longer and sickle-shaped. The almaco jack of the eastern Pacific is sometimes classified as a separate species, the Pacific amberjack (*Seriola colburni*).

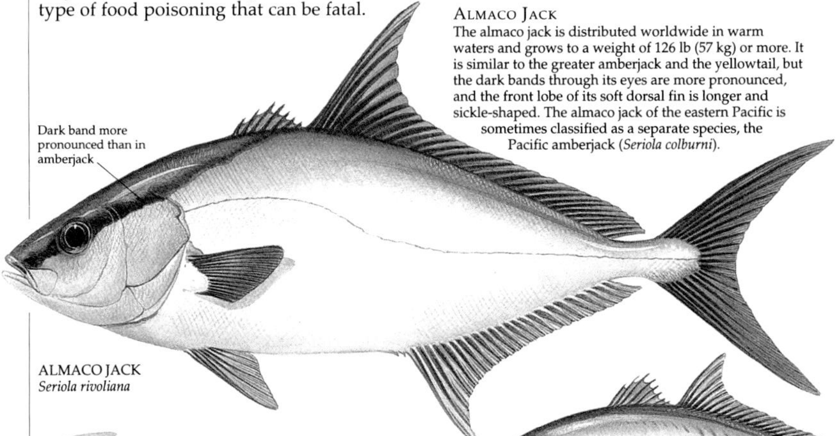

Dark band more pronounced than in amberjack

ALMACO JACK
Seriola rivoliana

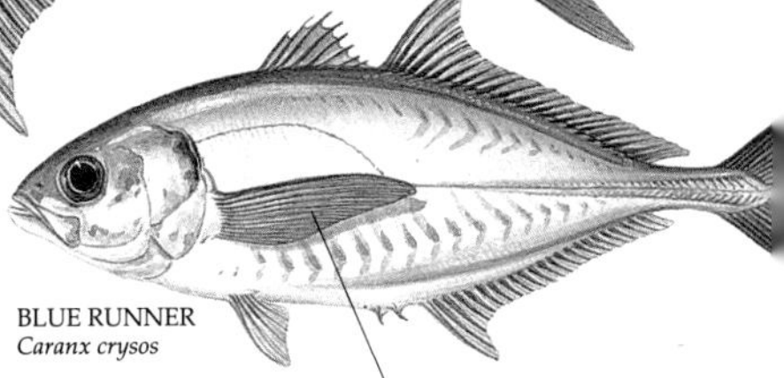

Schooling fish
Young fish of the Carangidae family often form small schools beneath floating objects such as jellyfish. Older fish of most species roam the seas in large, fast-swimming schools, but the oldest, largest fish tend to be solitary. The carangids are widely distributed in temperate and tropical seas, and are usually at their most abundant in inshore waters.

BLUE RUNNER
Caranx crysos

Large pectoral fin

BLUE RUNNER

The blue runner is a small Atlantic jack, very closely related to the Pacific green jack (*Caranx caballus*). It grows to over 8 lb (3.6 kg) but averages less than 1 lb (454 g); like most carangids, its flesh is tasty and it is fished for commercially. It is a popular angling species, and makes a very good bait for big-game fish.

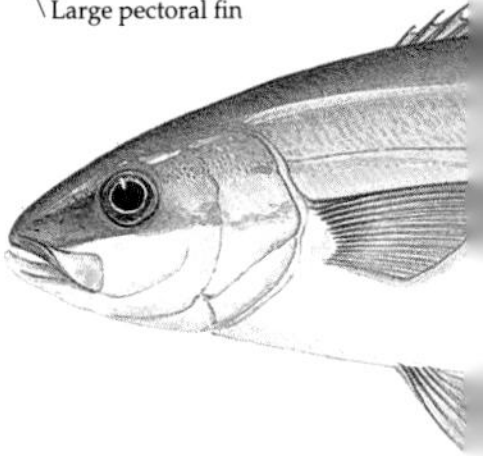

Size comparison

| Greater amberjack   Almaco jack   California yellowtail   Crevalle jack   Blue runner   Lesser amberjack

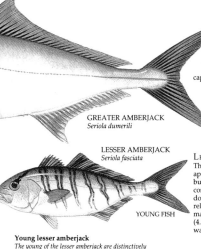

GREATER AMBERJACK
Seriola dumerili

LESSER AMBERJACK
Seriola fasciata

YOUNG FISH

Young lesser amberjack
The young of the lesser amberjack are distinctively marked with several broad, dark brown bands, usually separated by paler areas. These dark bands fade as the fish mature.

Large, domed head

Dark blotches

Faint yellow stripe

CALIFORNIA YELLOWTAIL
Seriola lalandi dorsalis

CALIFORNIA YELLOWTAIL
This subspecies of the yellowtail (*Seriola lalandi*) has a maximum weight of about 80 lb (36 kg), and is one of the most highly prized gamefish of the Pacific coast of North America. The closely related southern yellowtail, *S. grandis*, which is abundant in Australian and New Zealand waters, can reach a weight of 114 lb 10 oz (52 kg).

GREATER AMBERJACK
This fish is widely distributed in warm waters and is the largest amberjack in the Atlantic, averaging about 15 lb (6.8 kg) but capable of exceeding 176 lb (80 kg). Its overall coloration is silvery, and there is often a broad, yellow or coppery stripe along each side. The dark bands that run from its upper jaw through its first dorsal fin begins, forming an inverted V-shape.

LESSER AMBERJACK
The adult lesser amberjack is similar in appearance to the greater amberjack, but the dark bands on its head converge well in front of the first dorsal fin. The lesser amberjack is a relatively small fish, reaching a maximum weight of only about 10 lb (4.54 kg). It is found in the warm waters of the western Atlantic.

CREVALLE JACK
The hard-fighting crevalle jack is widely distributed in warm waters, and is found both inshore and in the open ocean. It averages under 2 lb (910 g), but can reach 55 lb (25 kg). The crevalle jack found in the Pacific is often regarded as a separate species, *Caranx caninus*; other Pacific and Indo-Pacific members of the genus *Caranx* include the trevally (*Caranx georgianus*), the ulua (*C. stellatus*), and the pauu'u (*C. ignobilis*).

CREVALLE JACK
Caranx hippos

DISTRIBUTION
Almaco jack: most tropical and warm-temperate waters.
Blue runner: tropical and warm-temperate Atlantic.
Greater amberjack: most tropical and warm-temperate waters.
Lesser amberjack: western Atlantic from Massachusetts south to Brazil.
Crevalle jack: most tropical and warm-temperate waters.
California yellowtail: eastern Pacific from British Columbia south to Chile.

FISHING NOTES

Techniques
Trolling, drifting, and spinning are the usual methods of fishing employed for amberjack and jack.

Tackle
For trolling and drifting, use a 30 lb (13.6 kg) class rod with a 4/0 baitcaster reel, 30 lb (13.6 kg) mono line, a wire or heavy mono leader, and a 6/0 or 8/0 single hook. For spinning, use a heavy spinning rod with a large spinning reel, 15 to 20 lb (6.8 to 9.1 kg) mono line, a wire leader, and a 4/0 or 6/0 single hook.

Bait
Chumming (groundbaiting) will attract and hold schools of fish near the boat. When trolling or drifting, use artificial lures, such as plugs and spinners, or natural baits such as squid and cut or whole fish. Good fish baits for these species include mullet, pinfish, sardines, and anchovies. For spinning, use plugs, spinners, or spoons.

Saltwater SPECIES

POMPANO, JACKMACKEREL, & ROOSTERFISH

The jackmackerel and the four species of pompano shown here (including the permit) are members of the Carangidae family, which also includes the amberjack and jack. The roosterfish is sometimes classified as a member of the Carangidae, but is usually placed in a separate family, the Nematistiidae. Pompano have deep, almost diamond-shaped bodies, while the jackmackerel and roosterfish are more elongated and streamlined. All except the African pompano venture close inshore, often into very shallow water within easy reach of shore anglers, and they offer good sport on light tackle.

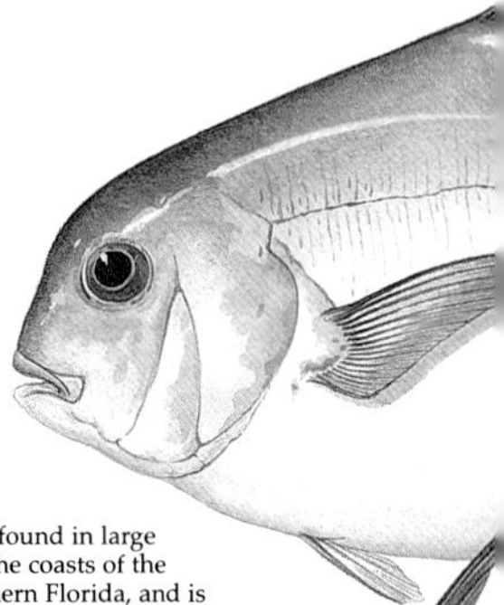

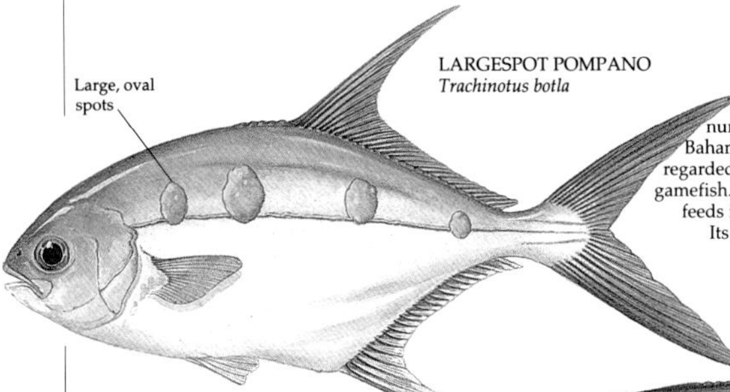

Large, oval spots

LARGESPOT POMPANO
Trachinotus botla

PERMIT
The permit is found in large numbers along the coasts of the Bahamas and southern Florida, and is regarded as one of the finest light-tackle gamefish. Like the bonefish (*see page 42*), it feeds in the shallow waters of coral flats. Its diet includes crabs, mollusks, shrimps, and sea urchins, and it grows to a weight of over 51 lb (23 kg).

JUVENILE PERMIT

LARGESPOT POMPANO
The largespot pompano is widely distributed in coastal waters of the Indian Ocean from Africa to Australia. It is found in the surf zones of sandy beaches, and when feeding it will often swim on its side so that it can move into very shallow water. It grows to a weight of more than 2 kg (4 lb 6 oz).

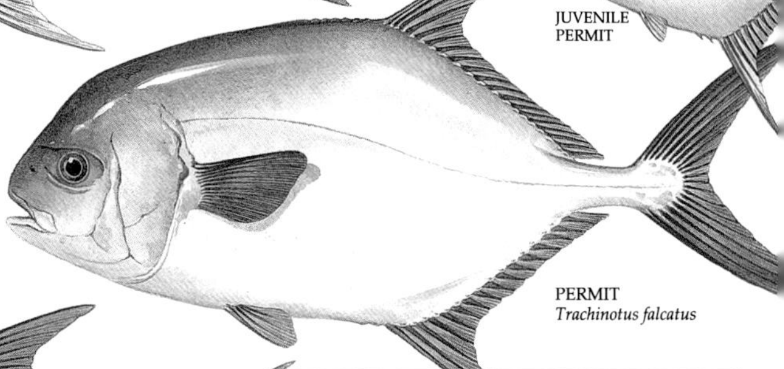

PERMIT
Trachinotus falcatus

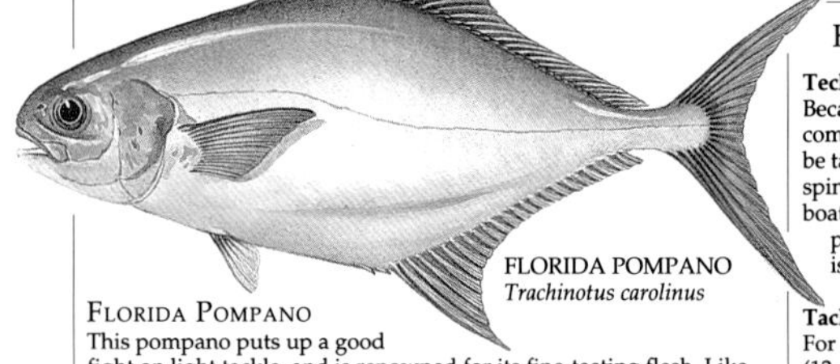

FLORIDA POMPANO
Trachinotus carolinus

FLORIDA POMPANO
This pompano puts up a good fight on light tackle, and is renowned for its fine-tasting flesh. Like the permit, it enters very shallow water, and is taken from beaches, piers, jetties, bridges, and drifting or anchored boats. It averages 910 g (2 lb), with a maximum weight of 3.6 kg (8 lb).

FISHING NOTES

Techniques
Because most of these species come close inshore, they can be taken by surfcasting or by spinning from the shore or a boat. The African pompano prefers deeper water and is caught by trolling.

Tackle
For surfcasting, try a 3.7 m (12 ft) rod that is capable of handling 85 to 142 g (3 to 5 oz) sinkers. For spinning and trolling, try a 2 to 2.4 m (6½ to 8 ft) medium spinning rod with 2.7 to 5.4 kg (6 to 12 lb) mono line, a short, 9.1 kg (20 lb) mono leader, and hook sizes 2 to 2/0.

Bait
The usual baits are crabs, clams, sand fleas, small bucktails, and jigs; anchovies are an excellent bait for jackmackerel.

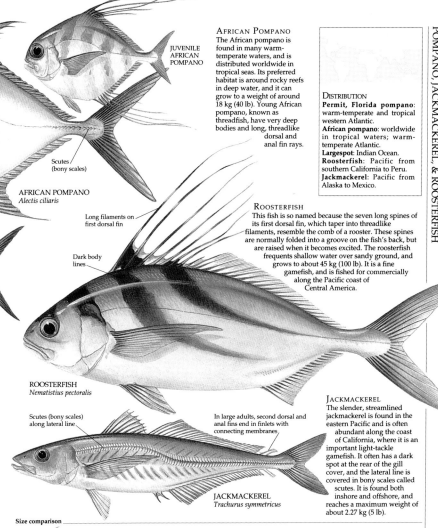

POMPANO, JACKMACKEREL, & ROOSTERFISH

AFRICAN POMPANO

The African pompano is found in many warm-temperate waters, and is distributed worldwide in tropical seas. Its preferred habitat is around rocky reefs in deep water, and it can grow to a weight of around 18 kg (40 lb). Young African pompano, known as threadfish, have very deep bodies and long, threadlike dorsal and anal fin rays.

JUVENILE AFRICAN POMPANO

Scutes (bony scales)

AFRICAN POMPANO
Alectis ciliaris

DISTRIBUTION
Permit, Florida pompano: warm-temperate and tropical western Atlantic.
African pompano: worldwide in tropical waters; warm-temperate Atlantic.
Largespot: Indian Ocean.
Roosterfish: Pacific from southern California to Peru.
Jackmackerel: Pacific from Alaska to Mexico.

Long filaments on first dorsal fin

Dark body lines

ROOSTERFISH

This fish is so named because the seven long spines of its first dorsal fin, which taper into threadlike filaments, resemble the comb of a rooster. These spines are normally folded into a groove on the fish's back, but are raised when it becomes excited. The roosterfish frequents shallow water over sandy ground, and grows to about 45 kg (100 lb). It is a fine gamefish, and is fished for commercially along the Pacific coast of Central America.

ROOSTERFISH
Nematistius pectoralis

JACKMACKEREL

The slender, streamlined jackmackerel is found in the eastern Pacific and is often abundant along the coast of California, where it is an important light-tackle gamefish. It often has a dark spot at the rear of the gill cover, and the lateral line is covered in bony scales called scutes. It is found both inshore and offshore, and reaches a maximum weight of about 2.27 kg (5 lb).

Scutes (bony scales) along lateral line

In large adults, second dorsal and anal fins end in finlets with connecting membranes

JACKMACKEREL
Trachurus symmetricus

Size comparison

Roosterfish   Permit   African pompano   Jackmackerel   Florida pompano   Largespot pompano

Saltwater SPECIES

COBIA, SNOOK, & BARRAMUNDI

The cobia, the only member of the Rachycentridae family, is a prized gamefish. It is also fished for commercially for its fine flesh, which is often sold smoked. Snook and barramundi belong to the Centropomidae family, which contains about 30 species. Some of the Centropomidae are exclusively marine, others are marine but move into brackish water and even into rivers; some live in rivers and spawn in brackish estuaries, while a few are found only in freshwater.

TARPON SNOOK
Centropomus pectinatus

Dark-tipped pelvic fin

COBIA
This long, slim-bodied fish occurs in most warm seas, from coastal waters to the open ocean, but is not found along the Pacific coast of North America. It has a flat head, a large mouth with a slightly protruding lower jaw, and a first dorsal fin that consists of eight separate spines. Fish and crustaceans make up the bulk of its diet, and it grows to a weight of about 150 lb (68 kg). It is usually solitary but sometimes forms small schools.

FAT SNOOK
The fat snook is a small, rather deep-bodied fish that rarely exceeds about 3 lb (1.36 kg). The most reliable way to distinguish it from other small snook is to count the number of scales along the lateral line: the fat snook has 80 to 90, the tarpon snook 65 to 70, and the black about 60.

FAT SNOOK
Centropomus parallelus

First dorsal fin reduced to eight spines

COBIA
Rachycentron canadum

FISHING NOTES

Techniques
Cobia are usually taken by bottom fishing with lures or natural baits. Lure fishing is an effective technique for barramundi and for snook, which can also be taken on fly tackle.

Tackle
For cobia, use a heavy spinning rod with 15 to 20 lb (6.8 to 9.1 kg) mono line and a 3 ft (90 cm) leader of wire or 60 to 80 lb (27.2 to 36.3 kg) mono, and hook sizes 2/0 to 4/0. Try a 6 ft (1.8 m) surfcaster with 10 to 12 lb (4.54 to 5.4 kg) mono line when

lure fishing for snook, and a fast, 9 ft (2.7 m) tip-action rod for fly fishing. For barramundi, use a 9 to 10 ft (2.7 to 3 m) spinning rod with 20 to 30 lb (9.1 to 13.6 kg) mono line.

Bait
Good baits for cobia include natural baits such as fish, crabs, and shrimps, and artificials including large plugs with bright blue or silver finishes, and 1½ to 3 oz (42 to 85 g) jigs with yellow or white skirts. Try plugs, spoons, jigs, shrimps, streamer flies, and fish (especially mullet) for snook, and jointed, 6 in (15 cm) shallow-diving plugs for barramundi.

Cobia habitat
Cobia like to lurk in the cover of pilings and wrecks, and beneath buoys, floating wreckage, and other flotsam. They are also often found in the company of cruising sharks.

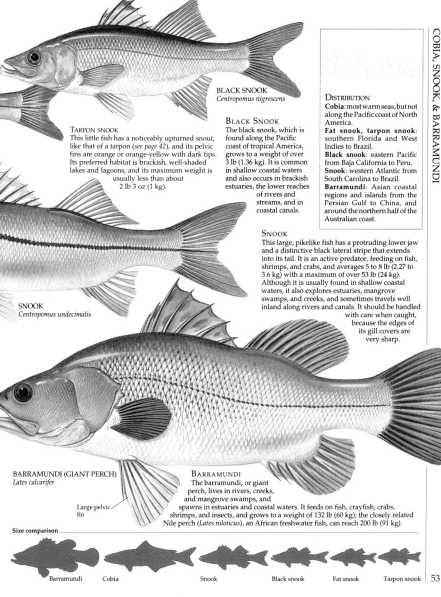

BLACK SNOOK
Centropomus nigrescens

TARPON SNOOK
This little fish has a noticeably upturned snout, like that of a tarpon (*see page 42*), and its pelvic fins are orange or orange-yellow with dark tips. Its preferred habitat is brackish, well-shaded lakes and lagoons, and its maximum weight is usually less than about 2 lb 3 oz (1 kg).

BLACK SNOOK
The black snook, which is found along the Pacific coast of tropical America, grows to a weight of over 3 lb (1.36 kg). It is common in shallow coastal waters and also occurs in brackish estuaries, the lower reaches of rivers and streams, and in coastal canals.

DISTRIBUTION
Cobia: most warm seas, but not along the Pacific coast of North America.
Fat snook, tarpon snook: southern Florida and West Indies to Brazil.
Black snook: eastern Pacific from Baja California to Peru.
Snook: western Atlantic from South Carolina to Brazil.
Barramundi: Asian coastal regions and islands from the Persian Gulf to China, and around the northern half of the Australian coast.

SNOOK
Centropomus undecimalis

SNOOK
This large, pikelike fish has a protruding lower jaw and a distinctive black lateral stripe that extends into its tail. It is an active predator, feeding on fish, shrimps, and crabs, and averages 5 to 8 lb (2.27 to 3.6 kg) with a maximum of over 53 lb (24 kg). Although it is usually found in shallow coastal waters, it also explores estuaries, mangrove swamps, and creeks, and sometimes travels well inland along rivers and canals. It should be handled with care when caught, because the edges of its gill covers are very sharp.

BARRAMUNDI (GIANT PERCH)
Lates calcarifer

Large pelvic fin

BARRAMUNDI
The barramundi, or giant perch, lives in rivers, creeks, and mangrove swamps, and spawns in estuaries and coastal waters. It feeds on fish, crayfish, crabs, shrimps, and insects, and grows to a weight of 132 lb (60 kg); the closely related Nile perch (*Lates niloticus*), an African freshwater fish, can reach 200 lb (91 kg).

Size comparison

Barramundi   Cobia   Snook   Black snook   Fat snook   Tarpon snook

SURFPERCH

The Embiotocidae family consists of 21 species, of which two occur in Japan and Korea; the rest are found along the Pacific coast of North America, and all but one are marine species. The exception is the tule perch (*Hysterocarpus traski*), a freshwater fish that has a limited distribution in central California. Surfperch males use their anal fins to transfer sperm to the females, which give birth to live young. Their food includes algae, invertebrates, and fish, and they range in length from 4 to 18 in (10 to 45 cm).

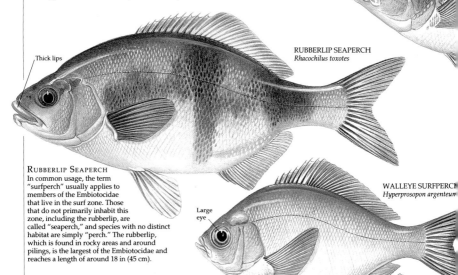

Thick lips

RUBBERLIP SEAPERCH
Rhacochilus toxotes

Large eye

WALLEYE SURFPERCH
Hyperprosopon argenteum

Black tip to pelvic fin

Breeding female has dark anal fin

RUBBERLIP SEAPERCH
In common usage, the term "surfperch" usually applies to members of the Embiotocidae that live in the surf zone. Those that do not primarily inhabit this zone, including the rubberlip, are called "seaperch," and species with no distinct habitat are simply "perch." The rubberlip, which is found in rocky areas and around pilings, is the largest of the Embiotocidae and reaches a length of around 18 in (45 cm).

WALLEYE SURFPERCH
The walleye surfperch is recognizable by its large eyes and its black-tipped pelvic fins, and its anal and tail fins often have dark edges. Its maximum length is about 12 in (30 cm), and it inhabits the surf zones of sandy beaches and is often found around piers. It is a very popular angling species and is of commercial importance.

FISHING NOTES

Techniques
Surfperch are usually caught by light surfcasting or by bottom fishing.

Tackle
For surfcasting, use a light surfcaster with a small baitcaster reel, 10 to 15 lb (4.54 to 6.8 kg) monofilament line, a size 1/0 hook (or smaller, depending on species sought),

and a grip or bomb-shaped sinker. For bottom fishing, try a spinning rod or a 12 lb (5.4 kg) class boat rod, fitted with a spinning reel or small baitcaster reel, 10 to 15 lb (4.54 to 6.8 kg) monofilament line, a size 1/0 hook (or smaller), and a bomb-shaped sinker.

Bait
Surfperch baits include cut fish and crab, ghost shrimps, clams, and mussels.

SHINER PERCH
This little surfperch, which grows to about 7 in (18 cm), is abundant and easily caught from piers, which makes it very popular with young anglers. Its habitat ranges from shallow water, where it frequents weedbeds, pilings, and piers, to depths of about 480 ft (146 m), and it will also venture into brackish areas and sometimes into freshwater. There is often a dark spot above its upper lip.

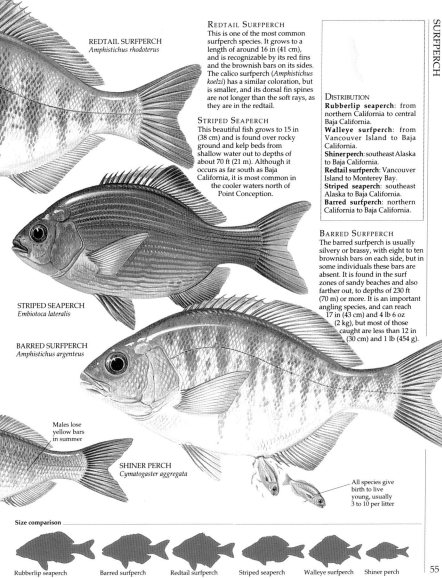

REDTAIL SURFPERCH
Amphistichus rhodoterus

REDTAIL SURFPERCH

This is one of the most common surfperch species. It grows to a length of around 16 in (41 cm), and is recognizable by its red fins and the brownish bars on its sides. The calico surfperch (*Amphistichus koelzi*) has a similar coloration, but is smaller, and its dorsal fin spines are not longer than the soft rays, as they are in the redtail.

STRIPED SEAPERCH

This beautiful fish grows to 15 in (38 cm) and is found over rocky ground and kelp beds from shallow water out to depths of about 70 ft (21 m). Although it occurs as far south as Baja California, it is most common in the cooler waters north of Point Conception.

DISTRIBUTION

Rubberlip seaperch: from northern California to central Baja California.
Walleye surfperch: from Vancouver Island to Baja California.
Shiner perch: southeast Alaska to Baja California.
Redtail surfperch: Vancouver Island to Monterey Bay.
Striped seaperch: southeast Alaska to Baja California.
Barred surfperch: northern California to Baja California.

BARRED SURFPERCH

The barred surfperch is usually silvery or brassy, with eight to ten brownish bars on each side, but in some individuals these bars are absent. It is found in the surf zones of sandy beaches and also farther out, to depths of 230 ft (70 m) or more. It is an important angling species, and can reach 17 in (43 cm) and 4 lb 6 oz (2 kg), but most of those caught are less than 12 in (30 cm) and 1 lb (454 g).

STRIPED SEAPERCH
Embiotoca lateralis

BARRED SURFPERCH
Amphistichus argenteus

Males lose yellow bars in summer

SHINER PERCH
Cymatogaster aggregata

All species give birth to live young, usually 3 to 10 per litter

Size comparison

Rubberlip seaperch   Barred surfperch   Redtail surfperch   Striped seaperch   Walleye surfperch   Shiner perch

GADIDAE

COD, HAKE, LING, & BURBOT

The members of the Gadidae, the codfish family, are distributed widely around the world, especially in the colder waters of the Northern Hemisphere. Most live at or near the bottom, feeding on fish and invertebrates, and many of them have great commercial importance as well as being popular quarry for sea anglers. Unfortunately, the commercial value of many species has led to serious overfishing in some areas, particularly the North Atlantic. As a result, there has been a serious decline in the numbers and sizes of these species.

Dark spot on flank behind gill cover

EUROPEAN POLLACK
Like many other members of the Gadidae, such as the Atlantic cod, this fish has three dorsal and two anal fins. It is most easily identified by its protruding lower jaw and the distinct curve of its lateral line. Small European pollack are found over sandy bottoms, but the larger ones, which can reach a weight of about 29 lb (13 kg), prefer rocky ground.

AMERICAN POLLACK
The American pollack is similar to the European, but its upper and lower jaws are approximately the same size, and its lateral line is only slightly curved. Its maximum size is about 71 lb (32 kg), and the largest individuals are usually found in the vicinity of reefs.

Heavily toothed jaw

EUROPEAN POLLACK
Pollachius pollachius

Downward-curving lateral line

AMERICAN POLLACK
Pollachius virens

Protruding lower jaw

BURBOT
This is the only member of the codfish family that lives exclusively in freshwater. It is widely distributed in deep, cold waters in northern latitudes, and although it averages about 2 lb (910 g) it can grow much larger, and specimens weighing in at around 71 lb (32 kg) have been taken from European waters. It is probably now extinct in the British Isles.

BURBOT
Lota lota

FISHING NOTES

Techniques
The marine codfish may be fished for from the shore by surfcasting or by fishing from rocks, piers, and jetties with natural baits, or from a boat with natural baits or by feathering, jigging (pirking), or using attractor spoons in conjunction with baited hooks. The burbot, the freshwater member of the codfish family, is a slow-moving fish that feeds mostly at night and may be caught by static legering in shallow water.

Tackle
When shore fishing for the marine species, try a 12 ft (3.7 m) surfcasting rod with a baitcaster reel, 30 lb (13.6 kg) nylon line, hook sizes 2/0 to 8/0, and a bomb-shaped or grip weight. To fish for the marine species from a boat, use a 30 lb (13.6 kg) class boat rod with a 4/0 to 6/0 baitcaster reel, 30 lb (13.6 kg) wire or nylon line, and hook sizes 2/0 to 8/0. When using natural baits and when feathering, use a bomb-shaped weight. For burbot, try a 10 to 12 ft (3 to 3.7 m) leger rod with a spinning reel, 6 lb (2.7 kg) mono line, and size 10 to 14 hook.

Bait
The wide range of effective natural baits for the marine species includes many invertebrates, such as mussels, lugworms, sandworms, razor clams, and squid. Fish baits, either cut or whole, are also worth trying, especially the oily fish such as herring, mackerel, sprat, and pilchard. Among the artificial baits, leadhead jigs, metal pirks, and plastic sandeels will get results, and a bunch of orange or white feather hackles on a 5/0 hook is excellent as a boat fishing lure. Burbot will take a bunch of large worms or a small fish.

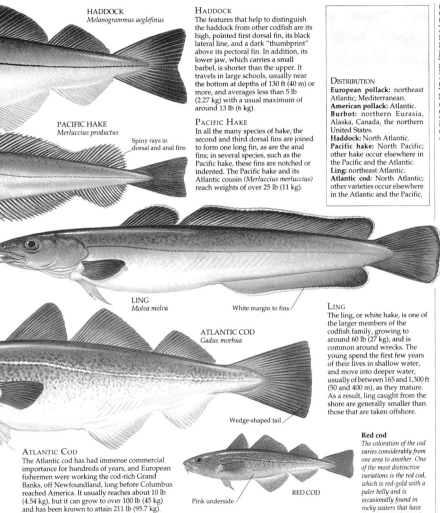

HADDOCK
Melanogrammus aeglefinus

PACIFIC HAKE
Merluccius productus

Spiny rays in
dorsal and anal fins

HADDOCK
The features that help to distinguish the haddock from other codfish are its high, pointed first dorsal fin, its black lateral line, and a dark "thumbprint" above its pectoral fin. In addition, its lower jaw, which carries a small barbel, is shorter than the upper. It travels in large schools, usually near the bottom at depths of 130 ft (40 m) or more, and averages less than 5 lb (2.27 kg) with a usual maximum of around 13 lb (6 kg).

PACIFIC HAKE
In all the many species of hake, the second and third dorsal fins are joined to form one long fin, as are the anal fins; in several species, such as the Pacific hake, these fins are notched or indented. The Pacific hake and its Atlantic cousin *(Merluccius merluccius)* reach weights of over 25 lb (11 kg).

DISTRIBUTION
European pollack: northeast Atlantic; Mediterranean.
American pollack: Atlantic.
Burbot: northern Eurasia, Alaska, Canada, the northern United States.
Haddock: North Atlantic.
Pacific hake: North Pacific; other hake occur elsewhere in the Pacific and the Atlantic.
Ling: northeast Atlantic.
Atlantic cod: North Atlantic; other varieties occur elsewhere in the Atlantic and the Pacific.

LING
Molva molva

White margin to fins

ATLANTIC COD
Gadus morhua

LING
The ling, or white hake, is one of the larger members of the codfish family, growing to around 60 lb (27 kg), and is common around wrecks. The young spend the first few years of their lives in shallow water, and move into deeper water, usually of between 165 and 1,300 ft (50 and 400 m), as they mature. As a result, ling caught from the shore are generally smaller than those that are taken offshore.

Wedge-shaped tail

Red cod
The coloration of the cod varies considerably from one area to another. One of the most distinctive variations is the red cod, which is red-gold with a paler belly and is occasionally found in rocky waters that have abundant weed growth.

ATLANTIC COD
The Atlantic cod has had immense commercial importance for hundreds of years, and European fishermen were working the cod-rich Grand Banks, off Newfoundland, long before Columbus reached America. It usually reaches about 10 lb (4.54 kg), but it can grow to over 100 lb (45 kg) and has been known to attain 211 lb (95.7 kg).

RED COD

Pink underside

Size comparison

Ling   Atlantic cod   European pollack   Haddock   Pacific hake   Burbot   American pollack   57

Saltwater SPECIES

BILLFISH & SWORDFISH

Highly prized by big-game anglers, the spectacularly hard-fighting billfish and swordfish roam widely through the world's tropical and warm-temperate seas, occasionally venturing into higher latitudes in summer. In all of these huge, fast-swimming fish – marlin, spearfish, sailfish, and swordfish – the upper jaw is elongated into a "bill" or "sword."

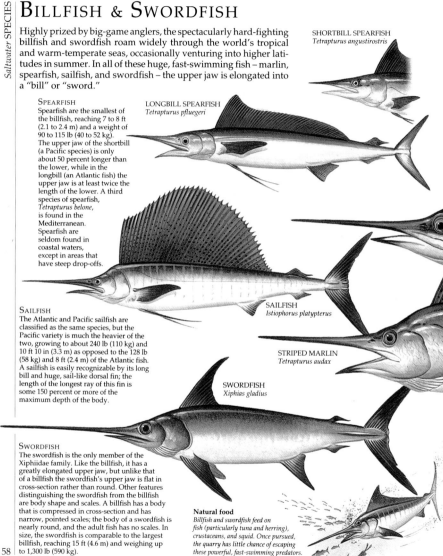

SHORTBILL SPEARFISH
Tetrapturus angustirostris

LONGBILL SPEARFISH
Tetrapturus pfluegeri

SPEARFISH

Spearfish are the smallest of the billfish, reaching 7 to 8 ft (2.1 to 2.4 m) and a weight of 90 to 115 lb (40 to 52 kg). The upper jaw of the shortbill (a Pacific species) is only about 50 percent longer than the lower, while in the longbill (an Atlantic fish) the upper jaw is at least twice the length of the lower. A third species of spearfish, *Tetrapturus belone*, is found in the Mediterranean. Spearfish are seldom found in coastal waters, except in areas that have steep drop-offs.

SAILFISH
Istiophorus platypterus

SAILFISH

The Atlantic and Pacific sailfish are classified as the same species, but the Pacific variety is much the heavier of the two, growing to about 240 lb (110 kg) and 10 ft 10 in (3.3 m) as opposed to the 128 lb (58 kg) and 8 ft (2.4 m) of the Atlantic fish. A sailfish is easily recognizable by its long bill and huge, sail-like dorsal fin; the length of the longest ray of this fin is some 150 percent or more of the maximum depth of the body.

STRIPED MARLIN
Tetrapturus audax

SWORDFISH
Xiphias gladius

SWORDFISH

The swordfish is the only member of the Xiphiidae family. Like the billfish, it has a greatly elongated upper jaw, but unlike that of a billfish the swordfish's upper jaw is flat in cross-section rather than round. Other features distinguishing the swordfish from the billfish are body shape and scales. A billfish has a body that is compressed in cross-section and has narrow, pointed scales; the body of a swordfish is nearly round, and the adult fish has no scales. In size, the swordfish is comparable to the largest billfish, reaching 15 ft (4.6 m) and weighing up to 1,300 lb (590 kg).

Natural food
Billfish and swordfish feed on fish (particularly tuna and herring), crustaceans, and squid. Once pursued, the quarry has little chance of escaping these powerful, fast-swimming predators.

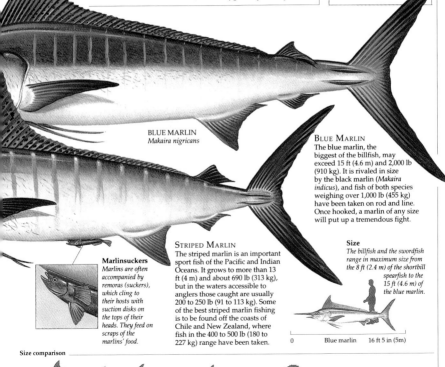

FISHING NOTES

Techniques

Trolling at or close to the surface is the usual technique for these species, but swordfish and blue marlin may also be taken by deep still-fishing using live or dead natural baits. In addition, the sailfish offers exciting sport to the saltwater fly fisherman. A billfish must be handled carefully when it is brought to the boat to be hauled on board or cut free, because the bill can inflict nasty wounds, and it is wise to wear gloves to protect your hands because the bill is very rough.

Tackle

For the smaller species, use a 20 to 50 lb (9.1 to 22.7 kg) class boat rod with a 20- to 50-class lever drag reel or a 6/0- or 7-class star drag reel. For larger fish use a 80 to 130 lb (36.3 to 59 kg) class rod with an 80- to 130-class lever drag or 12/0 or 14/0 star drag. Use 20 to 130 lb (9.1 to 59 kg) nylon or Dacron line with a heavy wire or nylon leader. Hooks should be flat-forged, 8/0 to 14/0. When fly fishing for sailfish, use a heavy fly rod with a suitable saltwater fly reel, a weight-forward #10 line with a 20 lb (9.1 kg) leader, and a streamer fly on a 2/0 to 5/0 hook.

Bait

Live or dead fish, such as mullet, mackerel, herring, and squid, and lures such as Kona Heads, feathered jigs, and plastic squids.

DISTRIBUTION

Blue marlin, sailfish and **swordfish**: worldwide.
Black and **striped marlins**: Pacific and Indian Oceans.
Shortbill spearfish: Pacific.
White marlin, longbill spearfish: Atlantic.

BLUE MARLIN
Makaira nigricans

BLUE MARLIN

The blue marlin, the biggest of the billfish, may exceed 15 ft (4.6 m) and 2,000 lb (910 kg). It is rivaled in size by the black marlin (*Makaira indicus*), and fish of both species weighing over 1,000 lb (455 kg) have been taken on rod and line. Once hooked, a marlin of any size will put up a tremendous fight.

Marlinsuckers

Marlins are often accompanied by remoras (suckers), which cling to their hosts with suction disks on the tops of their heads. They feed on scraps of the marlins' food.

STRIPED MARLIN

The striped marlin is an important sport fish of the Pacific and Indian Oceans. It grows to more than 13 ft (4 m) and about 690 lb (313 kg), but in the waters accessible to anglers those caught are usually 200 to 250 lb (91 to 113 kg). Some of the best striped marlin fishing is to be found off the coasts of Chile and New Zealand, where fish in the 400 to 500 lb (180 to 227 kg) range have been taken.

Size

The billfish and the swordfish range in maximum size from the 8 ft (2.4 m) of the shortbill spearfish to the 15 ft (4.6 m) of the blue marlin.

0   Blue marlin   16 ft 5 in (5m)

Size comparison

Blue marlin   Swordfish   Striped marlin   Sailfish   Longbill spearfish   Shortbill spearfish

Saltwater SPECIES

WRASSE & DOLPHINFISH

Wrasse belong to the Labridae family, which has more than 400 members distributed widely in coastal tropical and temperate waters. A typical wrasse has thick lips and strong teeth, which it uses to crush shellfish, and swims by flapping its pectoral fins rather than by using its tail. Wrasse range in size from small species about 4 in (10 cm) long up to the 7 ft 6 in (2.3 m) giant maori wrasse (*Cheilinus undulatus*) of Indo-Pacific waters. The dolphinfish is one of the two members of the Coryphaenidae family.

CALIFORNIA SHEEPHEAD
The coloration of the California sheephead varies with age and sex. Adult males are typically a striking black and red, but females are usually pinkish overall; both sexes have white throats. Young fish are red, with a dark spot on each fin. This wrasse is found along the coast of southern California, usually over rocky ground and kelp beds, at depths of about 10 to 180 ft (3 to 55 m). It grows to a maximum of around 3 ft (90 cm) and 36 lb 4 oz (16.4 kg).

SENORITA
Oxyjulis californica

SENORITA
This small, cigar-shaped fish inhabits kelp beds and rocky ground off the coast of southern California, and is best known to anglers as an expert bait stealer. It feeds on small invertebrates, and larger fish come to it to be cleaned of their parasites. Its maximum size is about 10 in (25 cm), and like many other small wrasse it buries itself in the sand at night.

FEMALE

MALE

CALIFORNIA SHEEPHEAD
Semicossyphus pulcher

MALE

DOLPHINFISH
The dolphinfish, also known as the dolphin or dorado, grows to about 88 lb (40 kg). Its diet consists mainly of fish (especially flying fish) plus squid and crustaceans, and it puts up a tremendous fight when hooked, making fast, powerful runs and leaping and tailwalking over the surface. The flesh of the dolphinfish is delicious, and is often sold under its Hawaiian name, *mahi mahi*. The much smaller pompano dolphin (*Coryphaena equisetis*), which resembles the female dolphinfish, reaches a weight of about 5 lb (2.27 kg).

DOLPHINFISH
Coryphaena hippurus

FISHING NOTES

Techniques
Most wrasse are taken by bottom fishing from the shore or cliffs. The usual techniques for dolphinfish are drift fishing, trolling, and spinning.

Tackle
For wrasse, try a 10 to 12 ft (3 to 3.7 m) light surfcasting or heavy spinning rod with 12 to 15 lb (5.4 to 6.8 kg) mono line. Terminal tackle should be a size 1/0 or 2/0

hook on a paternoster or running leger, with the sinker attached by a sacrificial weak link. For dolphinfish, try a heavy spinning rod or a 20 lb (9.1 kg) class boat rod, with 20 lb (9.1 kg) mono line and a 4/0 hook.

Bait
Wrasse will take a wide range of natural baits, including worms, crabs, mollusks, and crustaceans, and dolphinfish take fish, plugs, and spoons.

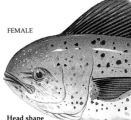

FEMALE

Head shape
The heads of female dolphinfish, and of young of both sexes, are more rounded than those of adult males.

60

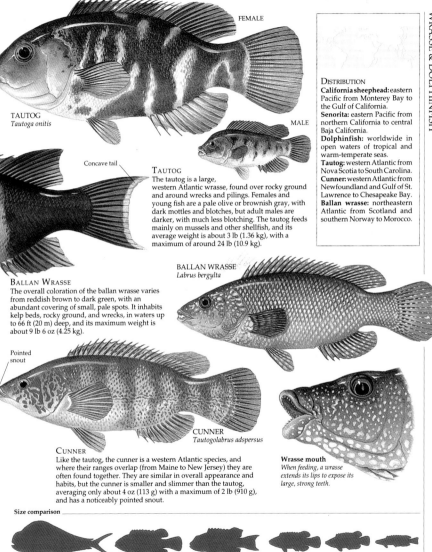

TAUTOG
Tautoga onitis

FEMALE

MALE

Concave tail

TAUTOG
The tautog is a large, western Atlantic wrasse, found over rocky ground and around wrecks and pilings. Females and young fish are a pale olive or brownish gray, with dark mottles and blotches, but adult males are darker, with much less blotching. The tautog feeds mainly on mussels and other shellfish, and its average weight is about 3 lb (1.36 kg), with a maximum of around 24 lb (10.9 kg).

California sheephead: eastern Pacific from Monterey Bay to the Gulf of California.
Senorita: eastern Pacific from northern California to central Baja California.
Dolphinfish: worldwide in open waters of tropical and warm-temperate seas.
Tautog: western Atlantic from Nova Scotia to South Carolina.
Cunner: western Atlantic from Newfoundland and Gulf of St. Lawrence to Chesapeake Bay.
Ballan wrasse: northeastern Atlantic from Scotland and southern Norway to Morocco.

BALLAN WRASSE
The overall coloration of the ballan wrasse varies from reddish brown to dark green, with an abundant covering of small, pale spots. It inhabits kelp beds, rocky ground, and wrecks, in waters up to 66 ft (20 m) deep, and its maximum weight is about 9 lb 6 oz (4.25 kg).

BALLAN WRASSE
Labrus bergylta

Pointed snout

CUNNER
Tautogolabrus adspersus

CUNNER
Like the tautog, the cunner is a western Atlantic species, and where their ranges overlap (from Maine to New Jersey) they are often found together. They are similar in overall appearance and habits, but the cunner is smaller and slimmer than the tautog, averaging only about 4 oz (113 g) with a maximum of 2 lb (910 g), and has a noticeably pointed snout.

Wrasse mouth
When feeding, a wrasse extends its lips to expose its large, strong teeth.

Size comparison

Dolphinfish   Tautog   California sheephead   Ballan wrasse   Cunner   Senorita

61

SNAPPER

Most of the 230 or so species of snapper that make up the Lutjanidae family are found in tropical seas, but a few also occur in warm-temperate waters. They are predatory fish, with sharp, conical teeth, including one or two large canine teeth on either side of the front of each jaw. These canine teeth help to distinguish the snappers from the groupers (*see page 84*), many species of which are similar in overall appearance. Large numbers of snapper are taken in shallow coastal waters and over reefs by anglers and spearfishers, and some species are fished for commercially.

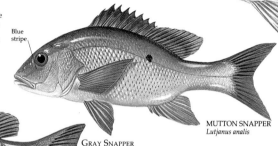

Long canine teeth

MUTTON SNAPPER
This is one of the most common snappers in the Caribbean and the waters off southern Florida, and is found near coral heads, in shallow channels and tidal creeks, on coral flats, and in blue holes – deep, circular holes or pits in the seabed. Its coloration is variable, but there is a blue stripe beneath each eye and a small dark spot on each side. Adults usually weigh from 5 to 10 lb (2.27 to 4.54 kg), and the maximum weight is about 25 lb (11.3 kg).

Blue stripe

MUTTON SNAPPER
Lutjanus analis

GRAY SNAPPER
The gray snapper, also known as the mangrove snapper, is found in the same waters as the mutton snapper and also occurs along the coast of tropical western Africa. It is most common along mangrove shores, but also lives over reefs, and grows to about 10 lb (4.54 kg). The overall coloration is grayish, sometimes tinged with red or copper, and there is often a dark stripe running from the snout through each eye.

GRAY SNAPPER
Lutjanus griseus

LANE SNAPPER
This little snapper is identifiable by its pink and yellow stripes, the black edge of its tail fin, and the large dark spot on each side between the dorsal fin and the lateral line. It is found in shallow water throughout the tropical west Atlantic, and although it usually weighs less than 1 lb (454 g), it is popular with anglers because it can be caught from piers and the shore and is good to eat.

LANE SNAPPER
Lutjanus synagris

FISHING NOTES

Techniques
Cubera, mutton snapper, and red snapper are taken by slow bottom trolling. Cubera and mutton snapper are also brought to the surface by chumming, and then taken by spinning with artificial lures. Spinning, with either artificial lures or natural baits, will take gray snapper, lane snapper, and river roman.

Tackle
For trolling, try a medium spinning rod with a spinning reel, 15 to 20 lb (6.8 to 9.1 kg) mono line, a 12 in (30 cm) wire or heavy mono leader, and a size 2/0 hook. For spinning, use a light or medium spinning rod with a baitcaster reel, 15 to 20 lb (6.8 to 9.1 kg) mono line, a 12 in (30 cm) wire or heavy mono leader (use transparent mono for gray snapper), and a size 2/0 treble hook.

Bait
Good natural baits for cubera, mutton, red, and lane snapper include shrimp and cut fish such as mullet. Artificial lures used for cubera snapper, mutton snapper, and river roman include bucktails, feathers, and jigs, and plugs with a flashy, silvery finish. These often work best when fished with a jerky retrieve. The best bait to use when fishing for gray snapper is live shrimp.

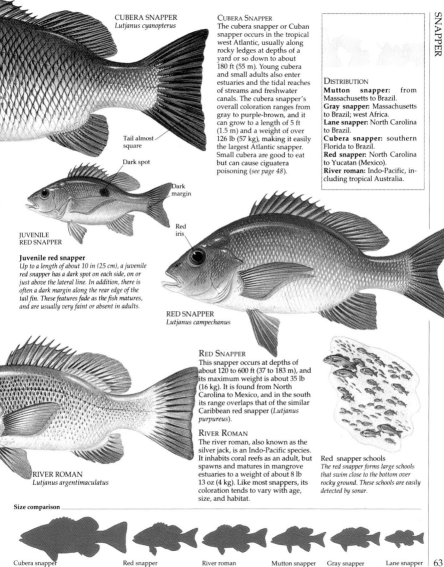

CUBERA SNAPPER
Lutjanus cyanopterus

Tail almost square

Dark spot

Dark margin

JUVENILE
RED SNAPPER

Dark margin

Red iris

Cubera Snapper
The cubera snapper or Cuban snapper occurs in the tropical west Atlantic, usually along rocky ledges at depths of a yard or so down to about 180 ft (55 m). Young cubera and small adults also enter estuaries and the tidal reaches of streams and freshwater canals. The cubera snapper's overall coloration ranges from gray to purple-brown, and it can grow to a length of 5 ft (1.5 m) and a weight of over 126 lb (57 kg), making it easily the largest Atlantic snapper. Small cubera are good to eat but can cause ciguatera poisoning (*see page 48*).

DISTRIBUTION
Mutton snapper: from Massachusetts to Brazil.
Gray snapper: Massachusetts to Brazil; west Africa.
Lane snapper: North Carolina to Brazil.
Cubera snapper: southern Florida to Brazil.
Red snapper: North Carolina to Yucatan (Mexico).
River roman: Indo-Pacific, including tropical Australia.

Juvenile red snapper
Up to a length of about 10 in (25 cm), a juvenile red snapper has a dark spot on each side, on or just above the lateral line. In addition, there is often a dark margin along the rear edge of the tail fin. These features fade as the fish matures, and are usually very faint or absent in adults.

RED SNAPPER
Lutjanus campechanus

Red Snapper
This snapper occurs at depths of about 120 to 600 ft (37 to 183 m), and its maximum weight is about 35 lb (16 kg). It is found from North Carolina to Mexico, and in the south its range overlaps that of the similar Caribbean red snapper (*Lutjanus purpureus*).

River Roman
The river roman, also known as the silver jack, is an Indo-Pacific species. It inhabits coral reefs as an adult, but spawns and matures in mangrove estuaries to a weight of about 8 lb 13 oz (4 kg). Like most snappers, its coloration tends to vary with age, size, and habitat.

Red snapper schools
The red snapper forms large schools that swim close to the bottom over rocky ground. These schools are easily detected by sonar.

RIVER ROMAN
Lutjanus argentimaculatus

Size comparison

Cubera snapper   Red snapper   River roman   Mutton snapper   Gray snapper   Lane snapper

Saltwater SPECIES

MULLET

There are about 70 species of mullet in the Mugilidae family, distributed worldwide in temperate and tropical waters. Most live close to the shore and often move into estuaries and rivers, and some, including the Australian mullet, inhabit freshwater. They are primarily bottom-feeders, living on algae, organic detritus, and small, mud-dwelling organisms, and are fished commercially as well as by anglers. The red mullet belongs to the Mullidae family (the goatfish), which consists of over 50 species widely distributed in warm waters.

STRIPED MULLET

This is one of the largest and most widely distributed of the mullet family, reaching a weight of about 15 lb (6.8 kg) and occurring in most warm seas. It is the only species of mullet found along the Pacific coast of North America. Its stripes are formed by horizontal rows of small dark spots, and there is a dark patch at the base of each pectoral fin. The origin of the second dorsal fin is in line with that of the anal fin.

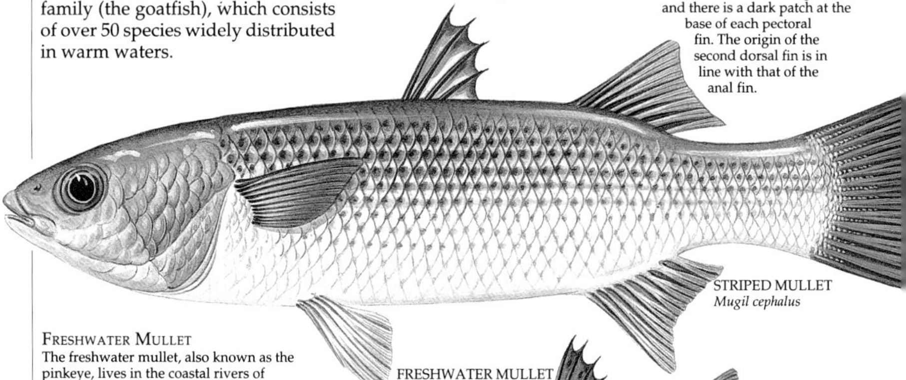

STRIPED MULLET
Mugil cephalus

FRESHWATER MULLET

The freshwater mullet, also known as the pinkeye, lives in the coastal rivers of southeast Australia, and migrates downstream to estuaries to spawn. It usually grows to about 16 in (40 cm), but can reach twice that length and a weight of 16 lb 8 oz (7.5 kg). Like marine mullet, it feeds mainly on algae and detritus.

FRESHWATER MULLET
Myxus petardi

Dark fins

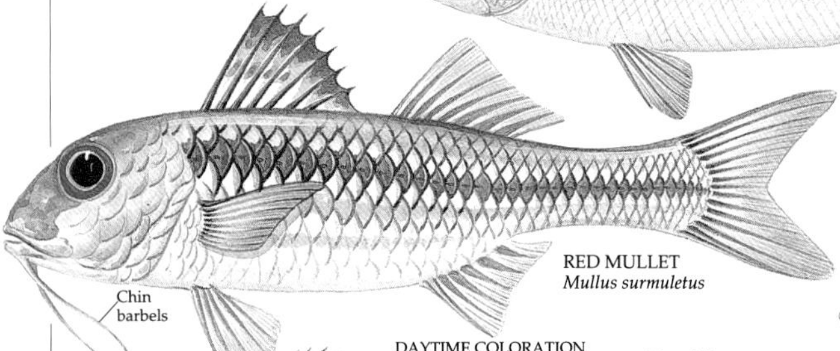

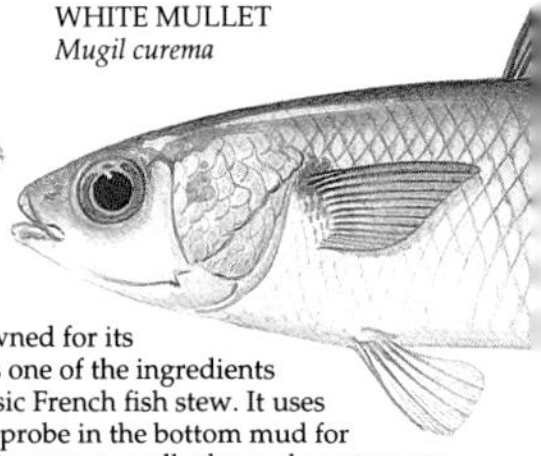

WHITE MULLET
Mugil curema

Chin barbels

RED MULLET
Mullus surmuletus

DAYTIME COLORATION

RED MULLET

The red mullet is renowned for its fine-tasting flesh and is one of the ingredients of *bouillabaisse*, the classic French fish stew. It uses its long chin barbels to probe in the bottom mud for its food, which is mainly worms, mollusks, and crustaceans, and at night its coloration changes from striped to mottled and barred. Its maximum weight is about 3 lb 10 oz (1.64 kg).

NIGHTTIME COLORATION

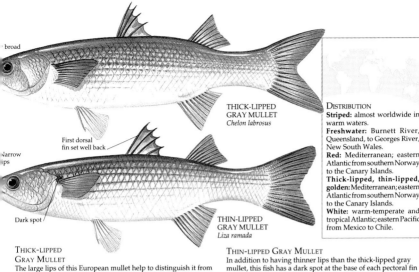

broad

THICK-LIPPED
GRAY MULLET
Chelon labrosus

First dorsal
fin set well back

Narrow
lips

Dark spot

THIN-LIPPED
GRAY MULLET
Liza ramada

DISTRIBUTION
Striped: almost worldwide in warm waters.
Freshwater: Burnett River, Queensland, to Georges River, New South Wales.
Red: Mediterranean; eastern Atlantic from southern Norway to the Canary Islands.
Thick-lipped, thin-lipped, golden: Mediterranean; eastern Atlantic from southern Norway to the Canary Islands.
White: warm-temperate and tropical Atlantic; eastern Pacific from Mexico to Chile.

THICK-LIPPED GRAY MULLET
The large lips of this European mullet help to distinguish it from the very similar thin-lipped gray mullet, which is found in the same waters where their ranges overlap. The thick-lipped gray mullet, which forms small schools that cruise near the surface, is found close inshore and enters harbors and estuaries. Its maximum weight is around 14 lb (6.4 kg).

GOLDEN MULLET
The golden mullet, sometimes called the golden gray mullet, resembles the thin-lipped gray but has an overall bronze hue and golden blotches on its cheeks. It is also smaller, with a maximum weight of under 3 lb (1.36 kg).

WHITE MULLET
This mullet is found in warm Atlantic waters and in the tropical eastern Pacific. It has a dark spot at the base of each pectoral fin, and often one or two gold patches on each side of its head. It usually grows to a weight of about 3 lb (1.36 kg).

THIN-LIPPED GRAY MULLET
In addition to having thinner lips than the thick-lipped gray mullet, this fish has a dark spot at the base of each pectoral fin and its first dorsal fin is set further back. Its habits are similar to those of the thick-lipped gray, but it is more likely to enter freshwater and is the most abundant mullet in European estuaries.   It grows to a maximum of about 7 lb (3.2 kg).

GOLDEN MULLET
Liza aurata

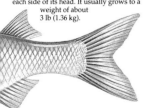

FISHING NOTES

Techniques
Float fishing, spinning, or freelining. These fish have soft, relatively small mouths and are easily spooked, so light tackle, delicate bait presentation, and a careful approach are required.

Tackle
Use a 10 to 12 ft (3 to 3.7 m) float rod for float fishing and freelining, with a spinning reel, 5 lb (2.27 kg) mono line, and hook sizes 6 to 16; for float fishing, use a peacock, Avon, or slider float and split shot. For spinning, try a 7 to 10 ft (2.1 to 3 m) light spinning rod with a spinning reel, 5 lb (2.27 kg) mono line, and size 10 treble hook.

Bait
Mullet will take a wide range of small, soft, natural and processed baits, including small or cut worms, maggots, banana, corn, cut fish, bread, cheese, peas, minced meat, and pasta. For spinning, use tiny spoons and spinners, baited with a small or cut sandworm.

Size comparison

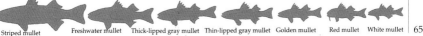

Striped mullet   Freshwater mullet   Thick-lipped gray mullet   Thin-lipped gray mullet   Golden mullet   Red mullet   White mullet

PLEURONECTIDAE; BOTHIDAE; SOLEIDAE

FLATFISH

For a few days after hatching from the egg, the larva of a flatfish resembles that of any other fish, but then it begins to change into the compressed, asymmetrical shape that makes flatfish superbly adapted to a bottom-hugging life. There are over 500 species, the main families being the Pleuronectidae or righteyed flatfish, in which both eyes are on the right side of the body; the Bothidae or lefteyed flatfish, in which both eyes are on the left; and the Soleidae or sole family, which contains mostly righteyed species.

PACIFIC HALIBUT
This huge, righteyed flatfish and its Atlantic counterpart (*Hippoglossus hippoglossus*) are among the largest fish in the sea, probably capable of exceeding 800 lb (360 kg). However, most caught by anglers are young fish weighing less than 10 lb (4.54 kg), the largest adults being found in very deep water.

SUMMER FLOUNDER
Paralichthys dentatus

Black and yellow bands on fins

Five prominent spots near tail

SUMMER FLOUNDER
This lefteyed flatfish reaches a weight of 26 lb (12 kg) and is usually marked with numerous ocelli (rimmed spots), of which five near the tail are large and prominent. It is found along the Atlantic coast of the United States, and from the Carolinas south its range overlaps that of the southern flounder (*Paralichthys lethostigma*), which is often marked with spots but not with ocelli.

STARRY FLOUNDER
Platichthys stellatus

STARRY FLOUNDER
This flatfish, which can be righteyed or lefteyed, is common on the Pacific coast of North America. Its fins are marked with black and yellow bands, and the upper side of its body has patches of shiny, star-shaped scales. It grows to 20 lb (9.1 kg), and hybridizes with the English sole (*Parophrys vetulus*) to produce the "hybrid sole."

SOLE
The sole, a common flatfish of the eastern Atlantic and the Mediterranean, is brown with dark patches on its upper side and creamy white below. It spends the day buried in the sand, feeding at night in midwater, and grows to 6 lb 10 oz (3 kg).

EUROPEAN PLAICE
Pleuronectes platessa

EUROPEAN PLAICE
The righteyed European plaice is found in the eastern Atlantic from the tidal shallows out to depths of about 650 ft (200 m). It is marked with bold red or orange spots and grows to a weight of over 10 lb (4.54 kg). The American plaice (*Hippoglossoides platessoides*) is similar, but lacks the red spotting and reaches 14 lb (6.4 kg).

SOLE
Solea solea

Eggs and larvae
Female flatfish lay up to 500,000 eggs. These float in the water, as do the symmetrically shaped larvae.

Size comparison

Pacific halibut   Turbot   Summer flounder   Starry flounder   Winter flounder   Plaice   Sole

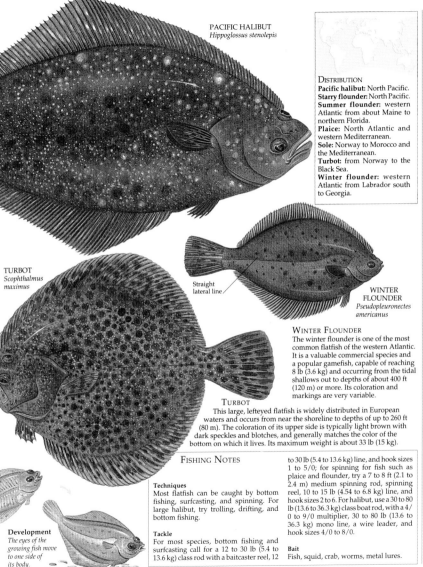

PACIFIC HALIBUT
Hippoglossus stenolepis

DISTRIBUTION
Pacific halibut: North Pacific.
Starry flounder: North Pacific.
Summer flounder: western Atlantic from about Maine to northern Florida.
Plaice: North Atlantic and western Mediterranean.
Sole: Norway to Morocco and the Mediterranean.
Turbot: from Norway to the Black Sea.
Winter flounder: western Atlantic from Labrador south to Georgia.

TURBOT
Scophthalmus maximus

Straight
lateral line

WINTER FLOUNDER
Pseudopleuronectes americanus

WINTER FLOUNDER
The winter flounder is one of the most common flatfish of the western Atlantic. It is a valuable commercial species and a popular gamefish, capable of reaching 8 lb (3.6 kg) and occurring from the tidal shallows out to depths of about 400 ft (120 m) or more. Its coloration and markings are very variable.

TURBOT
This large, lefteyed flatfish is widely distributed in European waters and occurs from near the shoreline to depths of up to 260 ft (80 m). The coloration of its upper side is typically light brown with dark speckles and blotches, and generally matches the color of the bottom on which it lives. Its maximum weight is about 33 lb (15 kg).

Development
The eyes of the growing fish move to one side of its body.

FISHING NOTES

Techniques
Most flatfish can be caught by bottom fishing, surfcasting, and spinning. For large halibut, try trolling, drifting, and bottom fishing.

Tackle
For most species, bottom fishing and surfcasting call for a 12 to 30 lb (5.4 to 13.6 kg) class rod with a baitcaster reel, 12 to 30 lb (5.4 to 13.6 kg) line, and hook sizes 1 to 5/0; for spinning for fish such as plaice and flounder, try a 7 to 8 ft (2.1 to 2.4 m) medium spinning rod, spinning reel, 10 to 15 lb (4.54 to 6.8 kg) line, and hook sizes 2 to 6. For halibut, use a 30 to 80 lb (13.6 to 36.3 kg) class boat rod, with a 4/0 to 9/0 multiplier, 30 to 80 lb (13.6 to 36.3 kg) mono line, a wire leader, and hook sizes 4/0 to 8/0.

Bait
Fish, squid, crab, worms, metal lures.

RAYS

The order Rajiformes consists of eight families of cartilaginous fish and includes the rays, mantas, sawfish, and skates (*see page 70*). These fish are characterized by flattened bodies and wide, often winglike, pectoral fins; their mouths and gill openings are on the undersides and their eyes are on the upper. In most families, the eggs are fertilized and hatch within the body of the female; the exception is the Rajidae, in which the internally fertilized eggs are laid before hatching.

MANTA

The mantas or devil rays belong to the Mobulidae family, which contains about a dozen species. These range in size from the Australian mobula (*Mobula diabola*), which measures about 2 ft (60 cm) across its wings, to the manta (*Manta birostris*), which reaches 22 ft (6.7 m) across the wings and a weight of 4,000 lb (1,820 kg). Despite its tremendous size, the manta is a generally harmless fish that feeds on small fish and crustaceans, which it steers into its mouth with its cephalic fins, the pair of "horns" on its head. Mantas cruise between midwater and the surface, and frequently leap into the air, perhaps to rid themselves of parasites or maybe just for fun.

THORNBACK RAY

The thornback is the most common ray in European waters. A member of the Rajidae family, it is a bottom-dweller found at depths of about 30 to 200 ft (10 to 60 m), and gets its name from the numerous thorny spines on its tail, back, and pectoral fins. Young thornbacks live in shallow water and feed on small crustaceans, and as they grow they move into deeper water and begin feeding on larger prey including crabs and fish. They grow to about 40 lb (18 kg).

SPOTTED RAY
Raja montagui

THORNBACK RAY
Raja clavata

Color variation
The color of the thornback is very variable, but most individuals are a mottled brown.

SPOTTED RAY

Like the thornback, the spotted ray is a European member of the Rajidae family. It lives in deeper water than the thornback, preferring depths of about 200 to 400 ft (60 to 120 m), and is a smaller fish, with a maximum weight of around 8 lb 6 oz (3.8 kg). Its diet consists mainly of crustaceans but it will also take small fish.

Spines
The thorny spines of the thornback and many other species have a strong, buttonlike base.

Egg cases
The eggs laid by members of the Rajidae family are each enclosed in a tough case known as a "mermaid's purse."

MANTA
Manta birostris

Size comparison

Atlantic manta

Sawfish

Bat ray

Thornback ray   Round stingray   Spotted ray

ROUND STINGRAY

The stingrays, members of the Dasyatidae family, have one or more venomous spines on their whiplike tails. Any wounds inflicted by the spines must get prompt medical attention because they can be fatal. The round stingray, measuring about 1 ft 10 in (56 cm) across the wings, is one of the smaller species; the Atlantic roughtail stingray (*Dasyatis centroura*) can be 7 ft (2.1 m) across.

Sharp spine can inflict painful wounds

ROUND STINGRAY
Urolophus halleri

LONGTOOTH SAWFISH
20 or fewer teeth

24 or more teeth

SMALLTOOTH SAWFISH

DISTRIBUTION

Manta: worldwide in warm-temperate and tropical waters.
Thornback ray: from Iceland to the Black Sea.
Spotted ray: from Scotland to the western Mediterranean.
Round stingray: from northern California to Panama.
Smalltooth sawfish: Mediterranean and warm-temperate and tropical Atlantic.
Bat ray: from Oregon to the Gulf of California.

SAWFISH

Sawfish (the Pristidae) are sharklike rays with elongated, flattened snouts that are equipped with rows of strong, sharp teeth along each side. The largetooth sawfish (*Pristis pristis*) and the smalltooth sawfish (*P. pectinata*) are Atlantic species that can reach weights of up to 800 lb (360 kg). Sawfish are also found in freshwater; for example, the largetooth sawfish is found 470 miles (750 km) up the Amazon.

SMALLTOOTH SAWFISH
Pristis pectinata

BAT RAY

The bat ray is a member of the Myliobatidae, the eagle ray family, which consists of about 30 species. They are large, free-swimming rays with distinct heads and very long tails, and feed on the bottom on shellfish and crustaceans. The bat ray grows to about 6 ft (1.8 m) across the wings.

BAT RAY
Myliobatis californica

FISHING NOTES

Techniques

Most rays live or feed on the bottom, so bottom fishing is the best technique. Manta usually feed at midwater or close to the surface, and are sometimes taken by trolling; they can be very dangerous and difficult to handle when hooked.

Tackle

For the thornback and spotted rays and the round stingray, use a heavy shore rod

or a 20 lb (9.1 kg) class boat rod, with a 4/0 to 6/0 baitcaster, 25 lb (11.3 kg) mono line and a 30 lb (13.6 kg) mono leader, size 2/0 to 4/0 hook, and a bomb-shaped weight. For sawfish and manta, try an 80 to 130 lb (36.3 to 59 kg) class rod with 80 to 130 lb (36.3 to 59 kg) mono line and a heavy wire or nylon leader, and size 8/0 to 14/0 hook.

Bait

Peeler crab, sandworms, and strips of fish such as mackerel.

Saltwater SPECIES

SKATES

The skates are members of the Rajidae (*see also page 68*), which contains over a hundred species and is the largest family within the order Rajiformes. Most skates are a mottled brownish color with whitish undersides, and their tails are relatively thick, rather than whiplike. Skates usually rest on the bottom during the day, lying partly buried in sand or mud, and become active at night to feed on shellfish, crustaceans, and sometimes small fish. They swim by making smooth undulations of their pectoral fins.

BIG SKATE
Raja binoculata

BARNDOOR SKATE
Raja laevis

BARNDOOR SKATE
This large, aggressive skate of the northwestern Atlantic grows to a length of around 5 ft (1.5 m) and a weight of 40 lb (18 kg). It is found from the tidal shallows out to depths of 1,410 ft (430 m), and will sometimes enter brackish water. It has a noticeably pointed snout, large, black pores on its underside, and a smooth skin. Its wings (pectoral fins) have concave leading edges and sharply angled corners. It feeds mainly on large crustaceans, mollusks, and fish such as herring, and it will readily take a baited hook.

Eye spot

BIG SKATE
The big skate, as its name indicates, is a large fish and can reach a length of 8 ft (2.4 m) and weigh over 200 lb (91 kg). It has a triangular snout, and there is a large eyespot on the upper surface of each wing. The big skate is found at depths of 10 to 360 ft (3 to 110 m) along the Pacific coast of North America, and the southern part of its range overlaps that of the California skate (*Raja inornata*). This skate is much smaller, about 2 ft 6 in (76 cm) long, with a sharply pointed snout and usually no eyespots.

Dark bars
and streaks

Sharp-angled corner
of wing

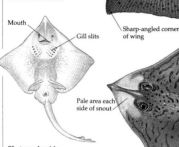

Mouth

Gill slits

CLEARNOSE SKATE
Raja eglanteria

Pale area each
side of snout

CLEARNOSE SKATE
The clearnose skate, which grows to a length of about 3 ft (90 cm), gets its name from the pale, translucent areas at either side of its snout. The overall coloration of its upper side is light brown to reddish brown, marked with dark bars, streaks, and spots. It migrates inshore to breed during the spring, and in summer it is the most abundant skate in the western Atlantic from Long Island to the Carolinas.

Skate underside
The underside of a skate is usually a pale, whitish color. The mouth is just below the snout, and just above the two sets of five gill slits.

Size comparison

Common skate   Big skate   Barndoor skate   Winter skate   Clearnose skate

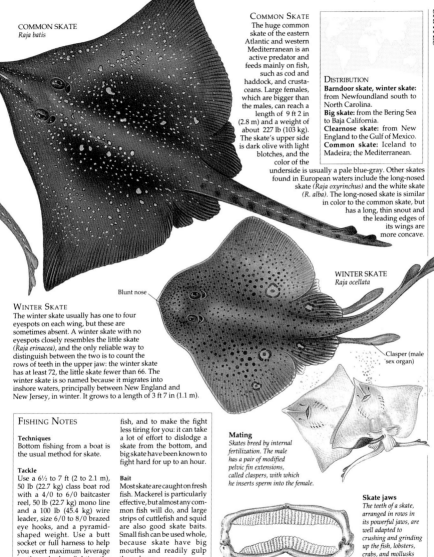

COMMON SKATE
Raja batis

COMMON SKATE

The huge common skate of the eastern Atlantic and western Mediterranean is an active predator and feeds mainly on fish, such as cod and haddock, and crustaceans. Large females, which are bigger than the males, can reach a length of 9 ft 2 in (2.8 m) and a weight of about 227 lb (103 kg). The skate's upper side is dark olive with light blotches, and the color of the underside is usually a pale blue-gray. Other skates found in European waters include the long-nosed skate (*Raja oxyrinchus*) and the white skate (*R. alba*). The long-nosed skate is similar in color to the common skate, but has a long, thin snout and the leading edges of its wings are more concave.

DISTRIBUTION

Barndoor skate, winter skate: from Newfoundland south to North Carolina.
Big skate: from the Bering Sea to Baja California.
Clearnose skate: from New England to the Gulf of Mexico.
Common skate: Iceland to Madeira; the Mediterranean.

WINTER SKATE
Raja ocellata

Blunt nose

WINTER SKATE

The winter skate usually has one to four eyespots on each wing, but these are sometimes absent. A winter skate with no eyespots closely resembles the little skate (*Raja erinacea*), and the only reliable way to distinguish between the two is to count the rows of teeth in the upper jaw: the winter skate has at least 72, the little skate fewer than 66. The winter skate is so named because it migrates into inshore waters, principally between New England and New Jersey, in winter. It grows to a length of 3 ft 7 in (1.1 m).

Clasper (male sex organ)

Mating
Skates breed by internal fertilization. The male has a pair of modified pelvic fin extensions, called claspers, with which he inserts sperm into the female.

FISHING NOTES

Techniques
Bottom fishing from a boat is the usual method for skate.

Tackle
Use a 6½ to 7 ft (2 to 2.1 m), 50 lb (22.7 kg) class boat rod with a 4/0 to 6/0 baitcaster reel, 50 lb (22.7 kg) mono line and a 100 lb (45.4 kg) wire leader, size 6/0 to 8/0 brazed eye hooks, and a pyramid-shaped weight. Use a butt socket or full harness to help you exert maximum leverage on the rod when fighting the fish, and to make the fight less tiring for you: it can take a lot of effort to dislodge a skate from the bottom, and big skate have been known to fight hard for up to an hour.

Bait
Most skate are caught on fresh fish. Mackerel is particularly effective, but almost any common fish will do, and large strips of cuttlefish and squid are also good skate baits. Small fish can be used whole, because skate have big mouths and readily gulp them down.

Skate jaws
The teeth of a skate, arranged in rows in its powerful jaws, are well adapted to crushing and grinding up the fish, lobsters, crabs, and mollusks that it feeds on.

DRUM & KAHAWAI

Saltwater SPECIES

The widely distributed Sciaenidae (drum) family consists of over 200 tropical and warm-temperate marine species – including drum, croaker, seatrout, seabass, and weakfish – plus the freshwater drum (*Aplodinotus grunniens*) of North America. Many species can make drumming sounds by contracting muscles on the walls of their swim bladders (gas-filled bladders that help to give them buoyancy). The kahawai, one of the two members of the Arripidae family, is also known as the Australian salmon because its juveniles bear a superficial resemblance to the Atlantic salmon.

BLACK DRUM
The black drum grows to a weight of over 115 lb (52 kg), and its deep body is marked with four or five dark bars on each side. It is a bottom feeder, and uses the barbels on its chin to help it locate the crustaceans and mollusks that make up the bulk of its diet. It is an important gamefish, commonly caught from the shore and piers.

RED DRUM
This large drum, also known as the redfish or channel bass, has a reddish overall coloration and one or more dark spots at the base of the tail. Its body is not as deep as that of the black drum, and it lacks chin barbels. It feeds at the bottom on crustaceans and mollusks and also takes small fish, especially mullet. The usual adult weight is under 40 lb (18 kg) but it can reach about 95 lb (43 kg).

RED DRUM
Sciaenops ocellatus

WHITE SEABASS
Atractoscion nobilis

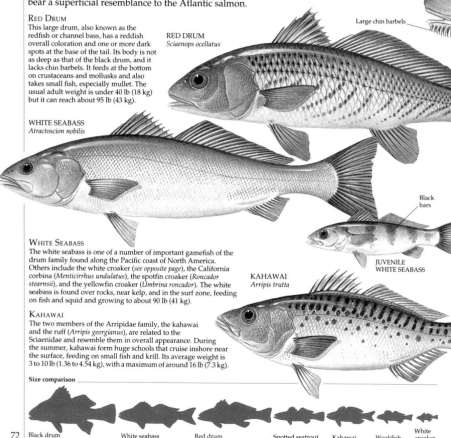

Large chin barbels

Black bars

JUVENILE WHITE SEABASS

KAHAWAI
Arripis trutta

WHITE SEABASS
The white seabass is one of a number of important gamefish of the drum family found along the Pacific coast of North America. Others include the white croaker (*see opposite page*), the California corbina (*Menticirrhus undulatus*), the spotfin croaker (*Roncador stearnsii*), and the yellowfin croaker (*Umbrina roncador*). The white seabass is found over rocks, near kelp, and in the surf zone, feeding on fish and squid and growing to about 90 lb (41 kg).

KAHAWAI
The two members of the Arripidae family, the kahawai and the ruff (*Arripis georgianus*), are related to the Sciaenidae and resemble them in overall appearance. During the summer, kahawai form huge schools that cruise inshore near the surface, feeding on small fish and krill. Its average weight is 3 to 10 lb (1.36 to 4.54 kg), with a maximum of around 16 lb (7.3 kg).

Size comparison

Black drum   White seabass   Red drum   Spotted seatrout   Kahawai   Weakfish   White croaker

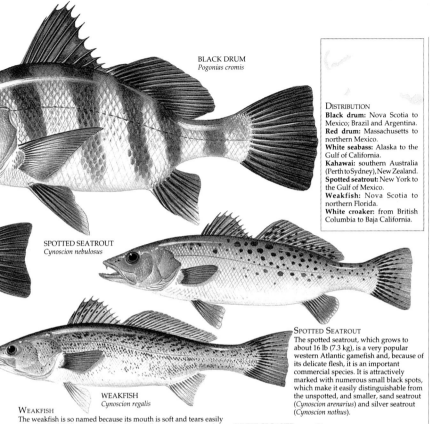

BLACK DRUM
Pogonias cromis

DISTRIBUTION
Black drum: Nova Scotia to Mexico; Brazil and Argentina.
Red drum: Massachusetts to northern Mexico.
White seabass: Alaska to the Gulf of California.
Kahawai: southern Australia (Perth to Sydney), New Zealand.
Spotted seatrout: New York to the Gulf of Mexico.
Weakfish: Nova Scotia to northern Florida.
White croaker: from British Columbia to Baja California.

SPOTTED SEATROUT
Cynoscion nebulosus

SPOTTED SEATROUT
The spotted seatrout, which grows to about 16 lb (7.3 kg), is a very popular western Atlantic gamefish and, because of its delicate flesh, it is an important commercial species. It is attractively marked with numerous small black spots, which make it easily distinguishable from the unspotted, and smaller, sand seatrout (*Cynoscion arenarius*) and silver seatrout (*Cynoscion nothus*).

WEAKFISH
Cynoscion regalis

WEAKFISH
The weakfish is so named because its mouth is soft and tears easily when hooked. It forms small schools in shallow water over sandy ground, and feeds at the bottom on worms, crustaceans, and mollusks, and in midwater and at the surface on small fish. Weakfish weighing over 19 lb (8.6 kg) have been caught, but the average size is declining and a weight of over 6 lb (2.7 kg) is rare.

WHITE CROAKER
Genyonemus lineatus

FISHING NOTES

Techniques
These fish are taken by a number of methods, the most usual being bottom fishing, surfcasting, and spinning.

Tackle
For bottom fishing, try a 30 lb (13.6 kg) class boat rod with a size 4/0 baitcaster reel, 30 lb (13.6 kg) mono line, size 4/0 hook, and a bomb-shaped sinker. When surfcasting, use a 12 ft (3.7 m) surfcasting rod with a spinning or baitcaster reel, 20 lb (9.1 kg) mono line, size 4/0 hook, and a grip sinker. For spinning, use an 8 to 9 ft (2.4 to 2.7 m) spinning rod with a spinning reel, 15 to 20 lb (6.8 to 9.1 kg) mono line, and size 1/0 to 4/0 hook.

Bait
Good baits include shrimp, fish, crab, clams, mussels, worms, and most types of artificial lure.

WHITE CROAKER
The white croaker is most reliably distinguished from other species of drum found along the Pacific coast of North America by the number of spines in its first dorsal fin: the white croaker has 12 to 16, the others 11 or fewer. It is found from close inshore to depths of 600 ft (183 m), and grows to about 1 lb (454 g).

73

MACKEREL

Saltwater SPECIES

The Scombridae family consists of about 45 species and includes the many species of mackerel, as well as tuna, bonito, and wahoo. The typical scombrid is a fast-swimming predator with a beautifully streamlined, spindle-shaped body and large, deeply forked or lunate (crescent-shaped) tail. Many scombrids are able to fold some of their fins into slots in their bodies to make them more streamlined and enable them to swim faster. The bluefin tuna, for example (*see page 77*), withdraws its pectoral, pelvic, and first dorsal fins in this way when traveling at speed.

CHUB MACKEREL

The chub mackerel or Pacific mackerel can reach a weight of 6 lb 5 oz (2.9 kg) but usually does not exceed 2 lb 3 oz (1 kg). It occurs in temperate and subtropical waters worldwide but its distribution is uneven, and there are minor differences between the Atlantic and Pacific varieties. Both, however, have widely separated first and second dorsal fins and about 30 wavy, dark bars on the back. This species is a very important commercial fish, especially in the Pacific region, and is found in large schools in inshore waters.

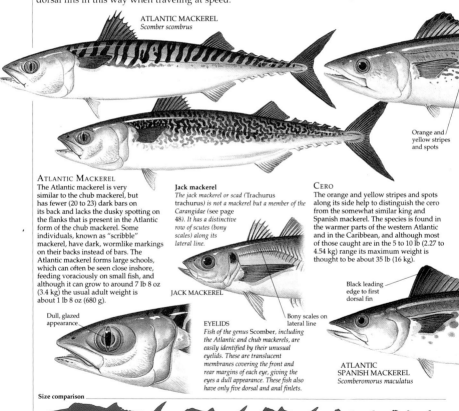

ATLANTIC MACKEREL
Scomber scombrus

Orange and yellow stripes and spots

ATLANTIC MACKEREL

The Atlantic mackerel is very similar to the chub mackerel, but has fewer (20 to 23) dark bars on its back and lacks the dusky spotting on the flanks that is present in the Atlantic form of the chub mackerel. Some individuals, known as "scribble" mackerel, have dark, wormlike markings on their backs instead of bars. The Atlantic mackerel forms large schools, which can often be seen close inshore, feeding voraciously on small fish, and although it can grow to around 7 lb 8 oz (3.4 kg) the usual adult weight is about 1 lb 8 oz (680 g).

Jack mackerel
The jack mackerel or scad (Trachurus trachurus) is not a mackerel but a member of the Carangidae (see page 48). It has a distinctive row of scutes (bony scales) along its lateral line.

JACK MACKEREL

CERO

The orange and yellow stripes and spots along its side help to distinguish the cero from the somewhat similar king and Spanish mackerel. The species is found in the warmer parts of the western Atlantic and in the Caribbean, and although most of those caught are in the 5 to 10 lb (2.27 to 4.54 kg) range its maximum weight is thought to be about 35 lb (16 kg).

Black leading edge to first dorsal fin

Dull, glazed appearance

EYELIDS
Fish of the genus Scomber, including the Atlantic and chub mackerels, are easily identified by their unusual eyelids. These are translucent membranes covering the front and rear margins of each eye, giving the eyes a dull appearance. These fish also have only five dorsal and anal finlets.

Bony scales on lateral line

ATLANTIC SPANISH MACKEREL
Scomberomorus maculatus

Size comparison

King mackerel   Cero   Spanish mackerel   Atlantic mackerel   Chub mackerel

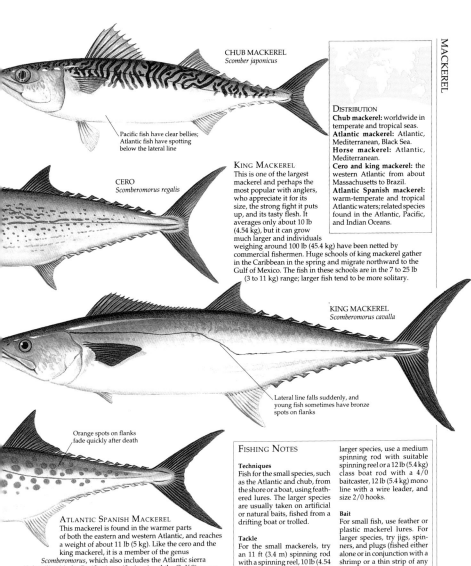

CHUB MACKEREL
Scomber japonicus

Pacific fish have clear bellies;
Atlantic fish have spotting
below the lateral line

CERO
Scomberomorus regalis

DISTRIBUTION
Chub mackerel: worldwide in temperate and tropical seas.
Atlantic mackerel: Atlantic, Mediterranean, Black Sea.
Horse mackerel: Atlantic, Mediterranean.
Cero and king mackerel: the western Atlantic from about Massachusetts to Brazil.
Atlantic Spanish mackerel: warm-temperate and tropical Atlantic waters; related species found in the Atlantic, Pacific, and Indian Oceans.

KING MACKEREL
This is one of the largest mackerel and perhaps the most popular with anglers, who appreciate it for its size, the strong fight it puts up, and its tasty flesh. It averages only about 10 lb (4.54 kg), but it can grow much larger and individuals weighing around 100 lb (45.4 kg) have been netted by commercial fishermen. Huge schools of king mackerel gather in the Caribbean in the spring and migrate northward to the Gulf of Mexico. The fish in these schools are in the 7 to 25 lb (3 to 11 kg) range; larger fish tend to be more solitary.

KING MACKEREL
Scomberomorus cavalla

Lateral line falls suddenly, and young fish sometimes have bronze spots on flanks

Orange spots on flanks fade quickly after death

ATLANTIC SPANISH MACKEREL
This mackerel is found in the warmer parts of both the eastern and western Atlantic, and reaches a weight of about 11 lb (5 kg). Like the cero and the king mackerel, it is a member of the genus *Scomberomorus*, which also includes the Atlantic sierra (*S. brasiliensis*), the Pacific sierra (*S. sierra*) and the Gulf Sierra or Monterey Spanish mackerel (*S. concolor*), both of which are Pacific species; and the Indo-Pacific mackerels *S. commerson* and *S. guttatus*, which are very common in Australian waters.

FISHING NOTES

Techniques
Fish for the small species, such as the Atlantic and chub, from the shore or a boat, using feathered lures. The larger species are usually taken on artificial or natural baits, fished from a drifting boat or trolled.

Tackle
For the small mackerels, try an 11 ft (3.4 m) spinning rod with a spinning reel, 10 lb (4.54 kg) line, a team of four lures with 1/0 hooks, and a 2 oz (57 g) bomb sinker. For the larger species, use a medium spinning rod with suitable spinning reel or a 12 lb (5.4 kg) class boat rod with a 4/0 baitcaster, 12 lb (5.4 kg) mono line with a wire leader, and size 2/0 hooks.

Bait
For small fish, use feather or plastic mackerel lures. For larger species, try jigs, spinners, and plugs (fished either alone or in conjunction with a shrimp or a thin strip of any common baitfish), and cut or whole baitfish such as mullet and balao.

TUNA & WAHOO

These members of the Scombridae family are widespread in temperate and tropical waters, and have considerable commercial importance as well as being important gamefish. The commercial value of tuna led to them being fished for with enormous driftnets, especially in the Pacific, but use of these nets has been restricted by international agreements because they took a heavy toll not only of tuna but also of unsought-for species including dolphins, sunfish, billfish, and Ray's bream.

ALBACORE
Because of its very long pectoral fins, which extend beyond the front of the anal fin, the albacore is also known as the longfin tuna. These fins help to distinguish the albacore from other tuna such as the bluefin. The Atlantic and the Pacific albacore were once considered to be separate species but are now known to be identical, and reach weights of around 95 lb (43 kg).

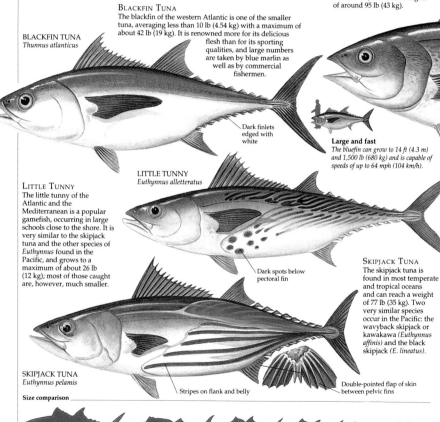

BLACKFIN TUNA
The blackfin of the western Atlantic is one of the smaller tuna, averaging less than 10 lb (4.54 kg) with a maximum of about 42 lb (19 kg). It is renowned more for its delicious flesh than for its sporting qualities, and large numbers are taken by blue marlin as well as by commercial fishermen.

BLACKFIN TUNA
Thunnus atlanticus

Dark finlets edged with white

Large and fast
The bluefin can grow to 14 ft (4.3 m) and 1,500 lb (680 kg) and is capable of speeds of up to 64 mph (104 km/h).

LITTLE TUNNY
The little tunny of the Atlantic and the Mediterranean is a popular gamefish, occurring in large schools close to the shore. It is very similar to the skipjack tuna and the other species of *Euthynnus* found in the Pacific, and grows to a maximum of about 26 lb (12 kg); most of those caught are, however, much smaller.

LITTLE TUNNY
Euthynnus alletteratus

Dark spots below pectoral fin

SKIPJACK TUNA
The skipjack tuna is found in most temperate and tropical oceans and can reach a weight of 77 lb (35 kg). Two very similar species occur in the Pacific: the wavyback skipjack or kawakawa (*Euthynnus affinis*) and the black skipjack (*E. lineatus*).

SKIPJACK TUNA
Euthynnus pelamis

Size comparison

Stripes on flank and belly

Double-pointed flap of skin between pelvic fins

Bluefin tuna   Wahoo   Albacore   Skipjack tuna   Little tunny   Blackfin tuna

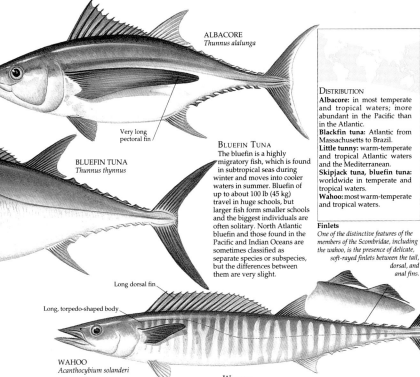

ALBACORE
Thunnus alalunga

Very long
pectoral fin

BLUEFIN TUNA
Thunnus thynnus

BLUEFIN TUNA
The bluefin is a highly migratory fish, which is found in subtropical seas during winter and moves into cooler waters in summer. Bluefin of up to about 100 lb (45 kg) travel in huge schools, but larger fish form smaller schools and the biggest individuals are often solitary. North Atlantic bluefin and those found in the Pacific and Indian Oceans are sometimes classified as separate species or subspecies, but the differences between them are very slight.

DISTRIBUTION
Albacore: in most temperate and tropical waters; more abundant in the Pacific than in the Atlantic.
Blackfin tuna: Atlantic from Massachusetts to Brazil.
Little tunny: warm-temperate and tropical Atlantic waters and the Mediterranean.
Skipjack tuna, bluefin tuna: worldwide in temperate and tropical waters.
Wahoo: most warm-temperate and tropical waters.

Finlets
One of the distinctive features of the members of the Scombridae, including the wahoo, is the presence of delicate, soft-rayed finlets between the tail, dorsal, and anal fins.

Long dorsal fin

Long, torpedo-shaped body

WAHOO
Acanthocybium solanderi

FISHING NOTES

Techniques
Trolling with lures and drift fishing with natural baits are the usual methods of fishing for tuna, little tunny, and albacore. When fishing for wahoo, try trolling with lures and natural baits, and drift fishing with natural baits. Wahoo are usually taken on flatlines that are fished quite near to the boat, rather than lines on outriggers.

Tackle
For tuna, use an 80 to 130 lb (36.3 to 59 kg) class rod with full roller rings, a lever drag multiplier, and 80 to 130 lb (36.3 to 59 kg) nylon line with a 400 to 600 lb (181 to 272 kg)

nylon leader. Use hook sizes 10/0 to 12/0, flat for trolling and offset for drifting. For wahoo, use a 30 to 50 lb (13.6 to 22.7 kg) class rod with a 6/0 star drag or 30- to 50-class baitcaster reel, 30 to 50 lb (13.6 to 22.7 kg) nylon line with a heavy wire leader, and a flat hook size 5/0 to 10/0.

Bait
Use a Kona Head lure when trolling for tuna, and try live mackerel or dead herring when drifting. When trolling for wahoo, use a Kona Head or other large artificial, or try a natural bait, such as a whole mullet or balao, mounted for trolling. For drift fishing, use a live baitfish on hook sizes 5/0 to 8/0.

WAHOO
The long, slender-bodied wahoo makes tremendous runs with abrupt changes of direction when hooked, sometimes leaping from the water, and this makes it one of the most exciting fish to catch. Its long, heavily toothed jaws form a beaklike snout, and its first dorsal fin is long, low, and spiny. The average weight is about 15 to 20 lb (6.8 to 9 kg), but it can grow to 183 lb (83 kg) and a length of 6 ft 11 in (2.1 m).

HEAD OF WAHOO

Wahoo jaws
The wahoo is a predatory fish (as are tuna), and its jaws contain rows of flat-sided, razor-sharp teeth that enable it to rip into squid and schools of baitfish. An unusual feature of the wahoo is that both its jaws are movable.

Saltwater SPECIES

BONITO & SHAD

Bonito, like mackerel and tuna (*see pages 74–77*), belong to the Scombridae famly. They are fast-swimming predators that feed on squid and small schooling fish, including mackerel, taken just below the surface. Shad, fish of the genus *Alosa*, are members of the herring family, the Clupeidae. They are marine fish that spawn in freshwater (some species also have landlocked populations), and differ from most other herring species in having a "keel" or "sawbelly", a ridge of sharp-edged scales along the belly.

PACIFIC BONITO
The Pacific bonito is a medium-sized fish that averages less than 12 lb (5.4 kg) but can grow to over 24 lb (11 kg). The northern and southern populations of the eastern Pacific are regarded as separate subspecies. Those north of Baja California are classified as *Sarda chiliensis lineolata*, and those off Peru and Chile as *S. c. chiliensis*. The striped bonito, *S. orientalis*, occurs from Baja to Peru, and in the western Pacific.

TWAITE SHAD
Alosa fallax

TWAITE SHAD
This shad differs from the Atlantic herring (*Clupea harengus*) in having a notch in its upper jaw, into which the lower jaw fits, a keel of sharp scales along its belly, and often has dark blotches along each side. Its maximum weight is about 3 lb 2 oz (1.4 kg).

ALLIS SHAD
Alosa alosa

AMERICAN SHAD
The American shad, which is capable of reaching a weight of over 12 lb (5.5 kg), has a large, dark spot behind each gill cover and usually one or two rows of dark spots along each side. It feeds almost entirely on plankton, and the adults have no jaw teeth.

ALLIS SHAD
The allis shad is similar to the twaite shad, but its keel is more pronounced and there may be a single dark blotch on each side, just behind the gill cover. It is also larger, reaching a weight of 6 lb (2.7 kg). Populations of both species have been severely depleted, mainly by pollution and damming of their spawning rivers.

Two rows of spots

AMERICAN SHAD
Alosa sapidissima

Shad diet
The diet of shad consists mainly of plankton, both animal and plant, plus insect larvae and copepods (tiny crustaceans). Skipjack herring and twaite, allis, and hickory shad also feed on small fish.

SKIPJACK HERRING
Alosa chrysochloris

FISHING NOTES

Techniques
Trolling and spinning for bonito, spinning and fly fishing for shad.

Tackle
To troll for bonito, use a 12 lb (5.4 kg) class boat rod with a size 2/0 baitcaster reel, 12 lb (5.4 kg) mono line, and a size 2/0 hook. When spinning for bonito, try a light spinning rod with a spinning reel, 12 lb (5.4 kg) line, and size 2/0 hook. To

spin for shad, use a light spinning rod with a spinning reel, 8 lb (3.6 kg) mono line, and small lures with treble hooks. For fly fishing, try a 9 ft (2.7 m) trout rod, weight-forward floating line, and flies tied on size 6 to 8 hooks.

Bait
For bonito, good baits include plugs, spoons, plastic squid, and whole or cut squid and fish. For shad, try small spinners and bar spoons, and small, white-colored flies.

SKIPJACK HERRING
The skipjack herring is also known as the river herring, and when in freshwater it prefers the open water of medium to large rivers and stillwaters. It is very similar to the hickory shad, but its flanks have a brassy tinge and no dark spots. Its maximum weight is about 3 lb 8 oz (1.6 kg).

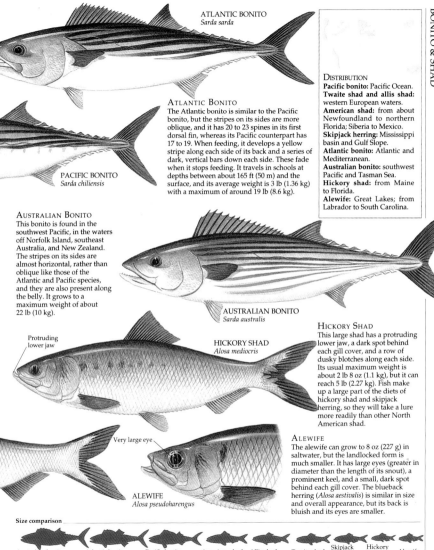

ATLANTIC BONITO
Sarda sarda

ATLANTIC BONITO
The Atlantic bonito is similar to the Pacific bonito, but the stripes on its sides are more oblique, and it has 20 to 23 spines in its first dorsal fin, whereas its Pacific counterpart has 17 to 19. When feeding, it develops a yellow stripe along each side of its back and a series of dark, vertical bars down each side. These fade when it stops feeding. It travels in schools at depths between about 165 ft (50 m) and the surface, and its average weight is 3 lb (1.36 kg) with a maximum of around 19 lb (8.6 kg).

DISTRIBUTION
Pacific bonito: Pacific Ocean.
Twaite shad and allis shad: western European waters.
American shad: from about Newfoundland to northern Florida; Siberia to Mexico.
Skipjack herring: Mississippi basin and Gulf Slope.
Atlantic bonito: Atlantic and Mediterranean.
Australian bonito: southwest Pacific and Tasman Sea.
Hickory shad: from Maine to Florida.
Alewife: Great Lakes; from Labrador to South Carolina.

PACIFIC BONITO
Sarda chiliensis

AUSTRALIAN BONITO
This bonito is found in the southwest Pacific, in the waters off Norfolk Island, southeast Australia, and New Zealand. The stripes on its sides are almost horizontal, rather than oblique like those of the Atlantic and Pacific species, and they are also present along the belly. It grows to a maximum weight of about 22 lb (10 kg).

AUSTRALIAN BONITO
Sarda australis

Protruding lower jaw

HICKORY SHAD
Alosa mediocris

HICKORY SHAD
This large shad has a protruding lower jaw, a dark spot behind each gill cover, and a row of dusky blotches along each side. Its usual maximum weight is about 2 lb 8 oz (1.1 kg), but it can reach 5 lb (2.27 kg). Fish make up a large part of the diets of hickory shad and skipjack herring, so they will take a lure more readily than other North American shad.

ALEWIFE
The alewife can grow to 8 oz (227 g) in saltwater, but the landlocked form is much smaller. It has large eyes (greater in diameter than the length of its snout), a prominent keel, and a small, dark spot behind each gill cover. The blueback herring (*Alosa aestivalis*) is similar in size and overall appearance, but its back is bluish and its eyes are smaller.

Very large eye

ALEWIFE
Alosa pseudoharengus

Size comparison

Australian bonito   Atlantic bonito   Pacific bonito   American shad   Allis shad   Twaite shad   Skipjack herring   Hickory shad   Alewife

SHARKS 1

The sharks are a very ancient group of fish, characterized by cartilaginous skeletons, skins covered in tiny, thornlike scales called placoid scales, five to seven gill slits, and powerful jaws equipped with rows of strong, sharp teeth. There are about 300 species, distributed widely throughout the world's seas but particularly in tropical waters, and although most are marine some enter estuaries, rivers, and creeks. They range in size from about 2 ft (60 cm) in length up to at least 60 ft (18 m); those shown here are among the smaller species, up to 11 ft 6 in (3.5 m) long.

PORBEAGLE
Lamna nasus

LEOPARD SHARK
This distinctively patterned shark occurs close inshore along the Pacific coast of the United States, and is especially common in the shallow bays of California. It is usually found in shallow, sandy-bottomed waters less than 12 ft (3.7 m) deep. Males grow to a length of 5 ft (1.5 m), and females reach 7 ft (2.1 m) and 71 lb (32 kg).

LEOPARD SHARK
Triakis semifasciata

Distinctive snout

TOPE
The tope is a member of the largest shark family, the Carcharhinidae or requiem sharks. It has a slender body and prominent snout, long pectoral fins, and a strong tail fin with a large lower lobe. It is found inshore in depths of about 10 ft (3 m) or more, and can attain a length of 5 ft 6 in (1.68 m) and a weight of 75 lb (34 kg). It feeds mainly on fish, such as cod, and also takes squid.

Large second dorsal fin

SMOOTH DOGFISH
Mustelus canis

SMOOTH DOGFISH
This very common, bottom-dwelling shark of the western Atlantic is usually found at depths of about 30 to 1,200 ft (9 to 360 m) and will sometimes enter freshwater. It has long pectoral fins and a large second dorsal fin that is almost the same size as the first, and there is a spiracle (a round opening that is the remnant of a first gill slit) behind each eye. It grows to about 5 ft (1.5 m).

Tope eyes
The eyes of the tope and most other requiem sharks have translucent membranes (nictitating membranes) that can be drawn across for protection.

Spiracle

Dorsal spines

TOPE
Galeorhinus galeus

SPURDOG
This slender shark, which grows to 4 ft (1.2 m) and 21 lb (9.5 kg), is unusual in having a sharp spine at the leading edge of each dorsal fin. Like the tope, it has a large, strong tail, but it has no anal fin. It lives just above the bottom in depths of about 30 to 650 ft (10 to 200 m), and it has a very varied diet consisting of schooling fish, such as herring, plus invertebrates such as squid, jellyfish, and worms.

SPURDOG
Squalus acanthias

Size comparison

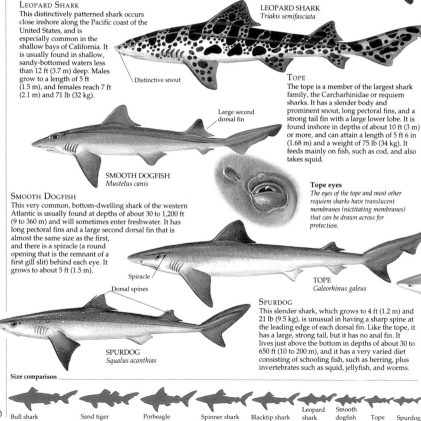

| Bull shark | Sand tiger | Porbeagle | Spinner shark | Blacktip shark | Leopard shark | Smooth dogfish | Tope | Spurdog |

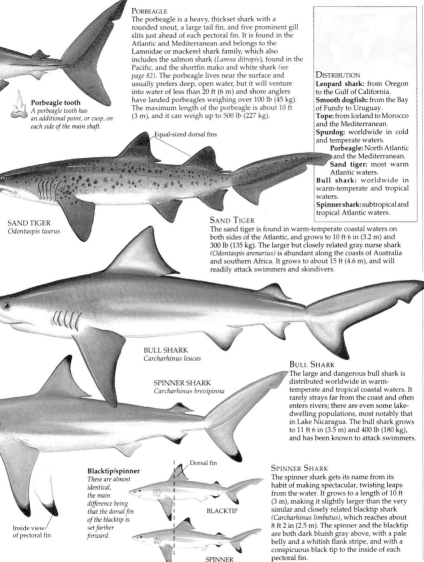

PORBEAGLE

The porbeagle is a heavy, thickset shark with a rounded snout, a large tail fin, and five prominent gill slits just ahead of each pectoral fin. It is found in the Atlantic and Mediterranean and belongs to the Lamnidae or mackerel shark family, which also includes the salmon shark (*Lamna ditropis*), found in the Pacific, and the shortfin mako and white shark (*see page 82*). The porbeagle lives near the surface and usually prefers deep, open water, but it will venture into water of less than 20 ft (6 m) and shore anglers have landed porbeagles weighing over 100 lb (45 kg). The maximum length of the porbeagle is about 10 ft (3 m), and it can weigh up to 500 lb (227 kg).

Porbeagle tooth
A porbeagle tooth has an additional point, or cusp, on each side of the main shaft.

DISTRIBUTION

Leopard shark: from Oregon to the Gulf of California.
Smooth dogfish: from the Bay of Fundy to Uruguay.
Tope: from Iceland to Morocco and the Mediterranean.
Spurdog: worldwide in cold and temperate waters.
Porbeagle: North Atlantic and the Mediterranean.
Sand tiger: most warm Atlantic waters.
Bull shark: worldwide in warm-temperate and tropical waters.
Spinner shark: subtropical and tropical Atlantic waters.

Equal-sized dorsal fins

SAND TIGER
Odontaspis taurus

SAND TIGER

The sand tiger is found in warm-temperate coastal waters on both sides of the Atlantic, and grows to 10 ft 6 in (3.2 m) and 300 lb (135 kg). The larger but closely related gray nurse shark (*Odontaspis arenarius*) is abundant along the coasts of Australia and southern Africa. It grows to about 15 ft (4.6 m), and will readily attack swimmers and skindivers.

BULL SHARK
Carcharhinus leucas

SPINNER SHARK
Carcharhinus brevipinna

BULL SHARK

The large and dangerous bull shark is distributed worldwide in warm-temperate and tropical coastal waters. It rarely strays far from the coast and often enters rivers; there are even some lake-dwelling populations, most notably that in Lake Nicaragua. The bull shark grows to 11 ft 6 in (3.5 m) and 400 lb (180 kg), and has been known to attack swimmers.

Blacktip/spinner
These are almost identical, the main difference being that the dorsal fin of the blacktip is set farther forward.

Dorsal fin

BLACKTIP

SPINNER

Inside view of pectoral fin

SPINNER SHARK

The spinner shark gets its name from its habit of making spectacular, twisting leaps from the water. It grows to a length of 10 ft (3 m), making it slightly larger than the very similar and closely related blacktip shark (*Carcharhinus limbatus*), which reaches about 8 ft 2 in (2.5 m). The spinner and the blacktip are both dark bluish gray above, with a pale belly and a whitish flank stripe, and with a conspicuous black tip to the inside of each pectoral fin.

Saltwater SPECIES

Sharks 2

The sharks shown here are representative of the larger species, and range in length from just under 13 ft (4 m) up to about 30 ft (9 m) or more. Not shown, because they are too big to be fished for, are the basking shark (*Cetorhinus maximus*) and whale shark (*Rhincodon typus*), huge but generally placid sharks that feed mainly on plankton. The basking shark is the largest shark in temperate waters, possibly growing to 45 ft (13.7 m) and 44,000 lb (20,000 kg); the whale shark, found in tropical seas, is the world's largest fish and may exceed 50 ft (15.2 m) and 77,000 lb (35,000 kg). The largest verified specimens of these two sharks were a 40 ft 3 in (12.27 m) basking shark and a 41 ft 6 in (12.65 m) whale shark.

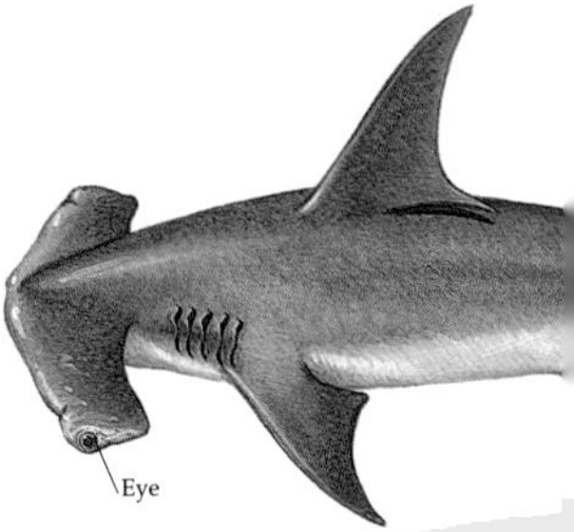

Eye

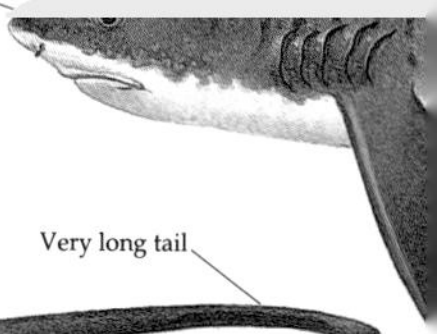

Blunt, very short snout

THRESHER SHARK
This warmwater shark is immediately recognizable by the exceptionally long upper lobe of its tail, which may be longer than its body. Threshers are found in the open ocean at depths from the surface down to 330 ft (100 m), and they grow to about 20 ft (6.1 m) and 1,000 lb (450 kg). They hunt in packs, using their tails to stun their prey.

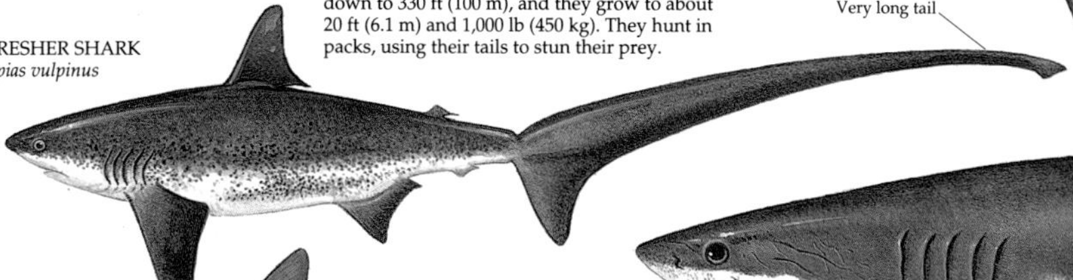

Very long tail

THRESHER SHARK
Alopias vulpinus

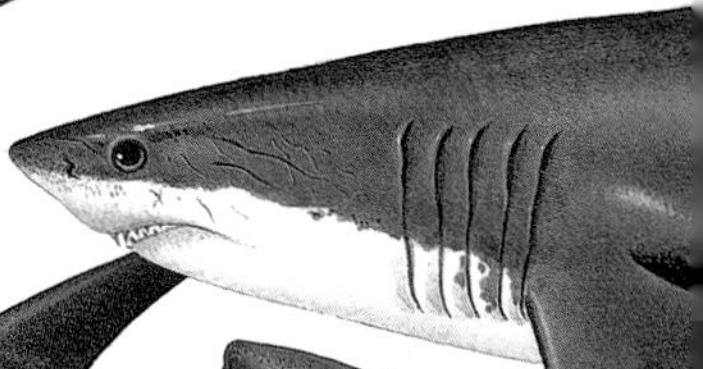

SHORTFIN MAKO
Isurus oxyrinchus

SHORTFIN MAKO
The shortfin mako, also known as the mako or bonito shark, is probably the fastest-swimming shark, capable of speed bursts of up to 46 mph (74 km/h). Its maximum size is about 12 ft 6 in (3.8 m) and 1,115 lb (506 kg), and it makes spectacular leaps when hooked.

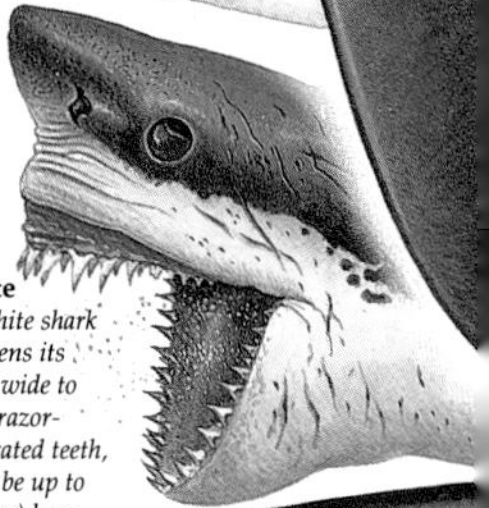

White shark bite
When a white shark bites, it opens its huge jaws wide to expose its razor-sharp, serrated teeth, which can be up to 3 in (7.6 cm) long.

SIXGILL SHARK
This large, bulky shark is identifiable by its single dorsal fin, which is set near the tail, and the six gill slits just ahead of each pectoral fin. The sixgill is found in temperate waters and lives at or near the bottom, the young in shallow water but the adults preferring depths of 250 ft (75 m) or more. It attains a size of at least 16 ft (4.9 m) and 1,300 lb (590 kg).

FISHING NOTES

Techniques
Trolling and drift fishing are the usual forms of shark fishing, but small sharks that venture into the inshore shallows are also taken by shore anglers, including saltwater fly fishers. Take care to avoid injury when handling sharks.

Tackle
When shore fishing for shark, try an 11 to 12 ft (3.4 to 3.7 m) rod with a baitcaster reel, 18 lb (8.2 kg) mono line with a wire leader, a 4 to 6 oz (113 to 170 g) weight, and hook sizes 4/0 to 6/0, or a medium to heavy saltwater fly outfit with a 12 in (30 cm) wire leader at the end of the tippet, and flies tied on 5/0 or 6/0 hooks. For trolling and drift fishing, the tackle depends on the size of shark you expect to catch. For example, a 20 lb (9.1 kg) class outfit should suffice for small species such as spurdog, but larger fish such as blue shark, porbeagle and mako require 50 to 80 lb (22.7 to 36.3 kg) class tackle.

Bait
Strips of fresh fish (such as mackerel or pollack) for small species, whole fish for the larger ones. For fly fishing, try white streamer flies.

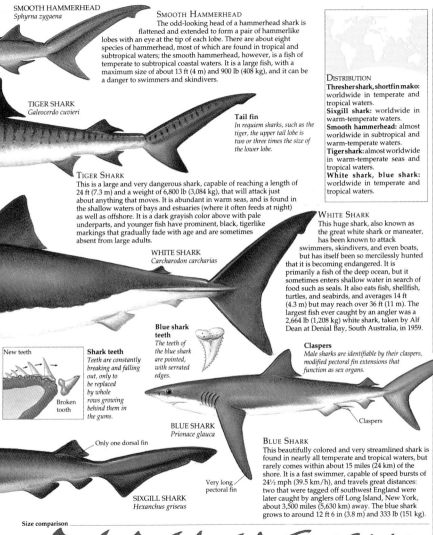

SMOOTH HAMMERHEAD
Sphyrna zygaena

SMOOTH HAMMERHEAD
The odd-looking head of a hammerhead shark is flattened and extended to form a pair of hammerlike lobes with an eye at the tip of each lobe. There are about eight species of hammerhead, most of which are found in tropical and subtropical waters; the smooth hammerhead, however, is a fish of temperate to subtropical coastal waters. It is a large fish, with a maximum size of about 13 ft (4 m) and 900 lb (408 kg), and it can be a danger to swimmers and skindivers.

DISTRIBUTION
Thresher shark, shortfin mako: worldwide in temperate and tropical waters.
Sixgill shark: worldwide in warm-temperate waters.
Smooth hammerhead: almost worldwide in subtropical and warm-temperate waters.
Tiger shark: almost worldwide in warm-temperate seas and tropical waters.
White shark, blue shark: worldwide in temperate and tropical waters.

TIGER SHARK
Galeocerdo cuvieri

Tail fin
In requiem sharks, such as the tiger, the upper tail lobe is two or three times the size of the lower lobe.

TIGER SHARK
This is a large and very dangerous shark, capable of reaching a length of 24 ft (7.3 m) and a weight of 6,800 lb (3,084 kg), that will attack just about anything that moves. It is abundant in warm seas, and is found in the shallow waters of bays and estuaries (where it often feeds at night) as well as offshore. It is a dark grayish color above with pale underparts, and younger fish have prominent, black, tigerlike markings that gradually fade with age and are sometimes absent from large adults.

WHITE SHARK
Carcharodon carcharias

WHITE SHARK
This huge shark, also known as the great white shark or maneater, has been known to attack swimmers, skindivers, and even boats, but has itself been so mercilessly hunted that it is becoming endangered. It is primarily a fish of the deep ocean, but it sometimes enters shallow water in search of food such as seals. It also eats fish, shellfish, turtles, and seabirds, and averages 14 ft (4.3 m) but may reach over 36 ft (11 m). The largest fish ever caught by an angler was a 2,664 lb (1,208 kg) white shark, taken by Alf Dean at Denial Bay, South Australia, in 1959.

Blue shark teeth
The teeth of the blue shark are pointed, with serrated edges.

New teeth

Shark teeth
Teeth are constantly breaking and falling out, only to be replaced by whole rows growing behind them in the gums.

Broken tooth

Claspers
Male sharks are identifiable by their claspers, modified pectoral fin extensions that function as sex organs.

Claspers

BLUE SHARK
Prionace glauca

BLUE SHARK
This beautifully colored and very streamlined shark is found in nearly all temperate and tropical waters, but rarely comes within about 15 miles (24 km) of the shore. It is a fast swimmer, capable of speed bursts of 24½ mph (39.5 km/h), and travels great distances: two that were tagged off southwest England were later caught by anglers off Long Island, New York, about 3,500 miles (5,630 km) away. The blue shark grows to around 12 ft 6 in (3.8 m) and 333 lb (151 kg).

Only one dorsal fin

Very long pectoral fin

SIXGILL SHARK
Hexanchus griseus

Size comparison

White shark   Tiger shark   Smooth hammerhead   Thresher shark   Sixgill shark   Shortfin mako   Blue shark

Saltwater SPECIES

GROUPER

The Serranidae is a large and important family of fish, consisting of more than 375 species. These are mostly temperate and tropical marine fish, ranging in size from less than 12 in (30 cm) to about 12 ft (3.7 m), and are found near rocks, reefs, wrecks, and piers in coastal waters. The larger members of the family are robust, sharp-toothed, basslike fish, which live near the bottom and feed on fish, crustaceans, and shellfish. They tend to be solitary rather than schooling, except at spawning time, and the individuals of many species change sex as they grow: they mature and breed as females, and become males when they grow older and larger.

YELLOWFIN GROUPER
This grouper has distinctive yellow tips to its pectoral fins, dark oval blotches on its head and body, and is speckled with small black spots. Its coloration is otherwise highly variable, but those in shallow water tend to be yellowish or green (yellow phase) and those in deep water red (red phase). Maximum weight is about 20 lb (9.1 kg).

RED PHASE

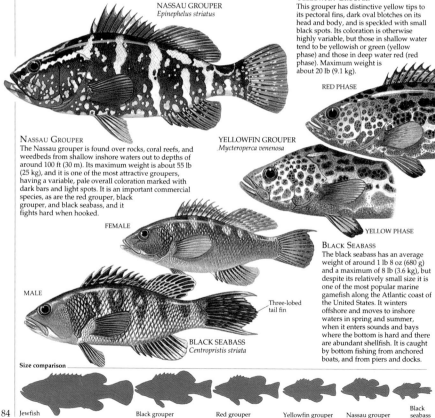

NASSAU GROUPER
Epinephelus striatus

NASSAU GROUPER
The Nassau grouper is found over rocks, coral reefs, and weedbeds from shallow inshore waters out to depths of around 100 ft (30 m). Its maximum weight is about 55 lb (25 kg), and it is one of the most attractive groupers, having a variable, pale overall coloration marked with dark bars and light spots. It is an important commercial species, as are the red grouper, black grouper, and black seabass, and it fights hard when hooked.

YELLOWFIN GROUPER
Mycteroperca venenosa

YELLOW PHASE

FEMALE

MALE

Three-lobed tail fin

BLACK SEABASS
Centropristis striata

BLACK SEABASS
The black seabass has an average weight of around 1 lb 8 oz (680 g) and a maximum of 8 lb (3.6 kg), but despite its relatively small size it is one of the most popular marine gamefish along the Atlantic coast of the United States. It winters offshore and moves to inshore waters in spring and summer, when it enters sounds and bays where the bottom is hard and there are abundant shellfish. It is caught by bottom fishing from anchored boats, and from piers and docks.

Size comparison

Jewfish   Black grouper   Red grouper   Yellowfin grouper   Nassau grouper   Black seabass

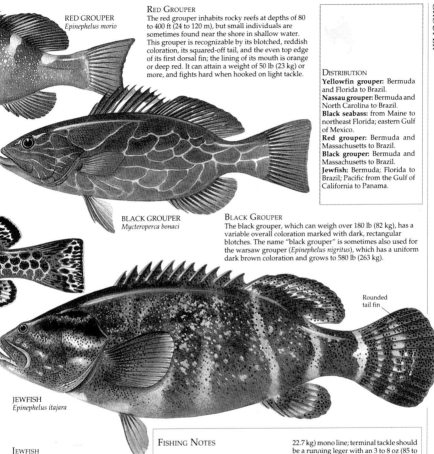

RED GROUPER
Epinephelus morio

RED GROUPER

The red grouper inhabits rocky reefs at depths of 80 to 400 ft (24 to 120 m), but small individuals are sometimes found near the shore in shallow water. This grouper is recognizable by its blotched, reddish coloration, its squared-off tail, and the even top edge of its first dorsal fin; the lining of its mouth is orange or deep red. It can attain a weight of 50 lb (23 kg) or more, and fights hard when hooked on light tackle.

DISTRIBUTION

Yellowfin grouper: Bermuda and Florida to Brazil.
Nassau grouper: Bermuda and North Carolina to Brazil.
Black seabass: from Maine to northeast Florida; eastern Gulf of Mexico.
Red grouper: Bermuda and Massachusetts to Brazil.
Black grouper: Bermuda and Massachusetts to Brazil.
Jewfish: Bermuda; Florida to Brazil; Pacific from the Gulf of California to Panama.

BLACK GROUPER
Mycteroperca bonaci

BLACK GROUPER

The black grouper, which can weigh over 180 lb (82 kg), has a variable overall coloration marked with dark, rectangular blotches. The name "black grouper" is sometimes also used for the warsaw grouper (*Epinephelus nigritus*), which has a uniform dark brown coloration and grows to 580 lb (263 kg).

Rounded tail fin

JEWFISH
Epinephelus itajara

JEWFISH

This huge grouper is known to reach a length of 8 ft (2.4 m) and a weight of 680 lb (310 kg), and may grow to 1,000 lb (454 kg) or more. Despite its size, it lives in shallow water – usually no deeper than 100 ft (30 m) – and is found around rocky ledges, wrecks, and pilings. It is not a hard fighter, but its size and weight, and its habit of bolting into a hole when hooked, make it difficult to land. The Queensland grouper (*Promicrops lanceolatus*), an Indo-Pacific species, is even larger and can grow to 12 ft (3.7 m) and over 1,100 lb (500 kg).

FISHING NOTES

Techniques

Bottom fishing and trolling, using natural or artificial baits, are effective methods for these species. Black seabass are also taken from jetties, docks, breakwaters, and piers on saltwater spinning gear and light, general-purpose tackle.

Tackle

For bottom fishing, use a 30 to 50 lb (13.6 to 22.7 kg) class boat rod with a 4/0 to 6/0 baitcaster reel and 30 to 50 lb (13.6 to 22.7 kg) mono line; terminal tackle should be a running leger with an 3 to 8 oz (85 to 227 g) pyramid- or bomb-shaped sinker and 2/0 to 6/0 hook. For trolling, try an 80 lb (36.3 kg) class rod with a 9/0 baitcaster reel, 80 lb (36.3 kg) mono line, a heavy wire leader and 10/0 hook.

Bait

Fish, squid, worms, shrimps, clams, and crab are good baits for bottom fishing. These natural baits can also be used for trolling, as can plugs, spinners, spoons, and feathers.

Saltwater SPECIES

PORGY & SEABREAM

Porgy and seabream are among the 120 species that make up the Sparidae family. The Sparidae have a worldwide distribution in temperate and tropical waters, but are most abundant in warm coastal seas. Most are small to medium-sized fish but some are quite large; in African waters, some species of steenbras (or musselcracker), such as *Pagrus nasutus* and *Petrus repuestris*, can grow to well over 120 lb (54 kg).

RED SEABREAM
The red seabream has red fins and a reddish tinge to its silvery body, and there is a large dark spot behind each gill cover. It is found in depths of 160 to 1,000 ft (50 to 300 m), particularly near reefs and wrecks, and feeds mainly on fish but also takes shrimps, crabs, and squid. Its maximum weight is about 10 lb (4.54 kg).

BLACK SEABREAM
This seabream is silvery gray overall, with a darker back, and usually has six or seven dark vertical bars on each side. Its maximum weight is around 7 lb (3.2 kg). The gilthead (*Sparus aurata*) is somewhat similar, but has a golden stripe across its forehead.

BLACK SEABREAM
Spondyliosoma cantharus

Dark spot

RED SEABREAM
Pagellus bogaraveo

Natural food
Fish make up the bulk of the red seabream's diet, but black seabream and most species of porgy feed mainly on mollusks and crustaceans.

SCUP
This small porgy, which grows to about 4 lb (1.8 kg), is a dull silvery gray overall, often with faint dark bars on its sides and sometimes a blue stripe at the base of its dorsal fin. The front teeth are sharp and incisor-like. The closely related longspine porgy (*Stenotomus caprinus*) is found from North Carolina to Florida and in the Gulf of Mexico.

SCUP
Stenotomus chrysops

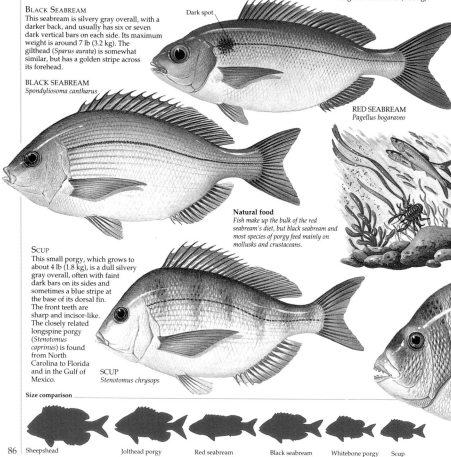

Size comparison

| Sheepshead | Jolthead porgy | Red seabream | Black seabream | Whitebone porgy | Scup |

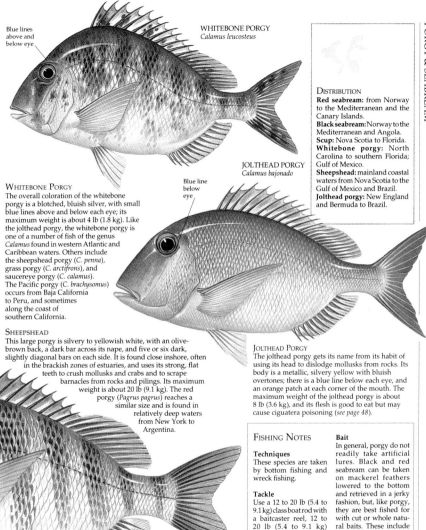

Blue lines above and below eye

WHITEBONE PORGY
Calamus leucosteus

DISTRIBUTION

Red seabream: from Norway to the Mediterranean and the Canary Islands.
Black seabream: Norway to the Mediterranean and Angola.
Scup: Nova Scotia to Florida.
Whitebone porgy: North Carolina to southern Florida; Gulf of Mexico.
Sheepshead: mainland coastal waters from Nova Scotia to the Gulf of Mexico and Brazil.
Jolthead porgy: New England and Bermuda to Brazil.

JOLTHEAD PORGY
Calamus bajonado

Blue line below eye

WHITEBONE PORGY

The overall coloration of the whitebone porgy is a blotched, bluish silver, with small blue lines above and below each eye; its maximum weight is about 4 lb (1.8 kg). Like the jolthead porgy, the whitebone porgy is one of a number of fish of the genus *Calamus* found in western Atlantic and Caribbean waters. Others include the sheepshead porgy (*C. penna*), grass porgy (*C. arctifrons*), and saucereye porgy (*C. calamus*). The Pacific porgy (*C. brachysomus*) occurs from Baja California to Peru, and sometimes along the coast of southern California.

SHEEPSHEAD

This large porgy is silvery to yellowish white, with an olive-brown back, a dark bar across its nape, and five or six dark, slightly diagonal bars on each side. It is found close inshore, often in the brackish zones of estuaries, and uses its strong, flat teeth to crush mollusks and crabs and to scrape barnacles from rocks and pilings. Its maximum weight is about 20 lb (9.1 kg). The red porgy (*Pagrus pagrus*) reaches a similar size and is found in relatively deep waters from New York to Argentina.

JOLTHEAD PORGY

The jolthead porgy gets its name from its habit of using its head to dislodge mollusks from rocks. Its body is a metallic, silvery yellow with bluish overtones; there is a blue line below each eye, and an orange patch at each corner of the mouth. The maximum weight of the jolthead porgy is about 8 lb (3.6 kg), and its flesh is good to eat but may cause ciguatera poisoning (*see page 48*).

SHEEPSHEAD
Archosargus probatocephalus

FISHING NOTES

Techniques
These species are taken by bottom fishing and wreck fishing.

Tackle
Use a 12 to 20 lb (5.4 to 9.1 kg) class boat rod with a baitcaster reel, 12 to 20 lb (5.4 to 9.1 kg) mono line, an 8 ft (2.4 m) single-hook leader or a two-hook bottom rig, and hook sizes from 6 to 2/0.

Bait
In general, porgy do not readily take artificial lures. Black and red seabream can be taken on mackerel feathers lowered to the bottom and retrieved in a jerky fashion, but, like porgy, they are best fished for with cut or whole natural baits. These include crab, shrimps, mussels, clams, worms, and sandeels, and strips of mackerel, cuttlefish, squid or octopus.

Saltwater SPECIES

SEA BREAM & SCORPION FISH

Sea bream – the Sparidae – have bodies that are compact, high-backed, compressed side-to-side, and covered in large, rough scales. They have very powerful dentition. Most are excellent swimmers and active predators, living in the surf along rocky coasts. Scorpion fish – the Scorpaenidae – have cylindrical bodies with numerous skin flaps and projections that give them superb camouflage. They are mainly nocturnal predators.

Gold marking

SALEMA
Sarpa salpa

HEAD
AND JAW
OF THE
GILT-HEAD

Powerful jaws
The gilt-head uses its extremely strong teeth to crush the shells of the mollusks that form its diet.

SALEMA
The salema fish lives in schools in coastal waters, often at shallow depth, feeding on a variety of algae. It is easily recognized by its oval body with gold bands along the sides. The small mouth points slightly downward.

SADDLED SEA BREAM
Oblada melanura

SCORPION FISH (RED)
Scorpaena scarfa

Swimming in shoals
The saddled sea bream swims in schools. These can be very large and are sometimes found patrolling near the surface.

Camouflage
Lying in wait for its prey, the scorpion fish is perfectly camouflaged by means of its many floating skin flaps and projections.

SCORPION FISH (BROWN)
Scorpaena porcus

SCORPION FISH (BROWN)
The dark coloring of the brown scorpion fish provides an even better disguise than that of its red counterpart. The fish lives among seaweed and stones in coastal waters, rarely going deeper than 100 ft (30.5 m). It makes excellent fish soup, but must be handled with care, as its fin spines can inflict painful wounds.

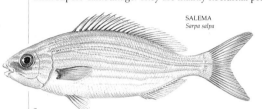

THE ANGLER'S NOTEBOOK

Techniques
Most sea bream species are actively sought out by anglers, especially the gilt-head, for which specific fishing techniques are used along the Mediterranean coast. The common two-banded sea bream and common pandora, with their delicious flesh, are also highly prized. These can be fished either from the shore or from a boat, with a floating line or by bait casting with small wigglers and spinners, with the line being suspended from a boat above the rocky beds where they like to hide. Ground bait is often needed to keep the school in one place.

Tackle
It is best to use a 16 to 20 ft (4.9 to 6 m) spin-casting rod or a strong bait-casting rod with 25 to 45/100 nylon thread on the spool.

Bait
Strips of squid, shellfish flesh, or slices of fish make the best bait.

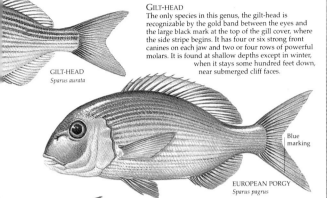

GILT-HEAD
The only species in this genus, the gilt-head is recognizable by the gold band between the eyes and the large black mark at the top of the gill cover, where the side stripe begins. It has four or six strong front canines on each jaw and two or four rows of powerful molars. It is found at shallow depths except in winter, when it stays some hundred feet down, near submerged cliff faces.

GILT-HEAD
Sparus aurata

Blue marking

EUROPEAN PORGY
Sparus pagrus

DISTRIBUTION
European porgy: Eastern Atlantic; Mediterranean.
Gilt-head: Eastern Atlantic; Mediterranean; Black Sea.
Common pandora: Eastern Atlantic; Mediterranean; Black Sea.
Salema: Eastern Atlantic; Mediterranean; Black Sea.
Scorpion fish: Atlantic; Mediterranean.
Common two-banded sea bream: Northeastern Atlantic; Mediterranean; Black Sea.
Saddled sea bream Eastern Atlantic.

COMMON TWO-BANDED SEA BREAM
Diplodus vulgaris

Black marking

EUROPEAN PORGY
The European porgy is recognizable by the slope of its profile, with a marked convex curve above the eye. It has powerful jaws, with a complex set of teeth, including four and six large canines in front and two rows of strong molars at the sides. The back is red or pink, in contrast with the silvery, pink-tinted flanks. In summer, the European porgy lives in inshore waters at depths of 30 to 100 ft (9.1 to 30.5 m). It feeds mainly on mollusks and crustaceans.

Wide black ring

SADDLED SEA BREAM
This is a free-swimming, mainly inshore species that sometimes forms large schools a few yards above the rocky or weedy bottoms that it favors. In winter it lives offshore. Its usual diet consists of algae and invertebrates. It is easy to identify from the black ring around its caudal peduncle and the thin gold-to-brown stripes along its silvery sides. It is rarely longer than 10–12 in (25.4–30.5 cm).

COMMON TWO-BANDED SEA BREAM
Rarely more than 16 in (40.5 cm)long, this magnificent fish is recognizable from two typical black markings, one behind the head and the other on the caudal peduncle. The dorsal fin is large, with numerous fin spines. The bulky body is oval in shape. The fish has an abundant set of teeth, including a second set of strong molars. The vigorous fight that it puts up makes it a favorite sporting fish.

COMMON PANDORA
This superb fish, with its characteristic orange-tinged livery and blue speckles on its sides, can also be recognized by the sloping curve of the head and the red mark on the upper edge of the gill cover. A gregarious fish, it lives in small schools on rocky or sandy bottoms at depths between 130 and 1,600 ft (40 and 488 m), in very specific places known to local fishermen. Most individuals start off as males and change into females at the age of two or three years.

COMMON PANDORA
Pagellus erythrinus

Size comparison

European porgy

Gilt-head

Common pandora

Salema

Scorpion fish (red)

Scorpion fish (brown)

Common two-banded sea bream

Saddled sea bream

GLOSSARY

A

Adipose fin A small, fatty fin between the dorsal fin and the tail fin.

AFTMA The American Fishing Tackle Manufacturers Association. Its activities include setting technical standards for fishing tackle, and its fly tackle specifications have become the world standard.

Alevin A recently hatched salmon or trout (*see also* **Grilse, Kelt, Parr, Smolt**).

Algae Any of a number of groups of simple plants that contain chlorophyll but lack true roots, stems, and leaves. They live in water or moist ground, and include diatoms, seaweeds, and spirogyra.

Amphidromous fish Fish that regularly migrate between freshwater and saltwater for reasons other than spawning, for example to feed or to overwinter (*see also* **Anadromous fish, Catadromous fish, Potamodromous fish**).

Anadromous fish Fish that spend most of their lives in the sea but ascend rivers to spawn (*see also* **Amphidromous fish, Catadromous fish, Potamodromous fish**).

Anal fin The fin behind the anus of a fish.

Aorta The main artery carrying blood from the heart.

Articular The rear bone of the lower jaw of a fish. It is hinged to the upper jaw and the quadrate (*see also* **Dentary, Maxillary, Premaxillary, Quadrate**).

B

Bag limit The maximum permissible number or weight of fish that can be taken from a particular water: always check local regulations before fishing.

Baitfish Any small fish, such as minnows and sandeels, that are preyed on by larger species and commonly used as angling bait.

Baiting needle A long needle used for mounting dead fish and other large baits onto terminal tackle.

Banks The right bank of a river is on your right when you are facing downstream, and the left bank is on your left.

Basin A depression in the Earth's surface; the drainage basin of a river system; a very large depression in the Earth's surface, containing an ocean and the rivers that drain into it, for example the Pacific Basin (*see also* **Drainage basin**).

Benthic A term describing anything living at or near the bottom of a lake or the sea.

Biomass The total mass of all the living organisms in a given area or in a given body of water (aquatic biomass).

Bowfishing Fishing with a bow and arrow. It is permitted on many American waters, and the quarry is usually "trash" fish (such as carp) that are competing with more highly prized species such as bass. The arrow is tied to the end of the line, and the reel is mounted on the bow.

Brackish water Water that is slightly salty (*see also* **Salinity**).

Breaking strain The maximum load or weight that a line, swivel, or other piece of tackle can sustain without breaking.

b.s. The abbreviation for breaking strain.

Bulk shot A number of split shot grouped together on a line to concentrate weight at a particular point.

Butt pad A leather or rubber pad, strapped around the waist, into which the butt of a rod is placed so that greater leverage can be exerted when fighting large, powerful fish. It is also known as a rod socket (*see also* **Fighting chair**).

C

Caeca See **Pyloric caeca**

Catadromous fish Freshwater fish that move to the lower river or sea to spawn (*see also* **Amphidromous fish, Anadromous fish, Potamodromous fish**).

Caudal peduncle The relatively slender part of a fish's body between the last dorsal and anal fins and the base of the tail fin (the caudal fin). It is also known as the "wrist" of the fish.

Cleithrum A bone at the rear of the skull of a fish. It is the main bone supporting the pectoral fin (*see also* **Pectoral fin, Supracleithrum**).

Coarse fish Any freshwater fish of angling interest other than gamefish and panfish (*see also* **Gamefish, Panfish**).

D

Deadbait Dead fish or other creatures used as bait for predators (*see also* **Livebait**).

Dead drift A fly-fishing technique in which the fly (dry or wet) is allowed to drift freely along in the current.

Demersal fish Fish that live in deep water or on the sea floor (*see also* **Pelagic fish**).

Dentary The front bone of the lower jaw of a fish (*see also* **Articular, Maxillary, Premaxillary, Quadrate**).

Deoxygenation Reduction in the dissolved oxygen content of a water, caused by hot weather or the introduction of pollutants such as sewage. Excessive deoxygenation is fatal to fish.

Detritus Accumulated silt and organic debris on the bed of a river or stillwater.

Disturbance pattern A wet- or dry-fly pattern that creates a fish-attracting disturbance when retrieved or worked across the current (*see also* **Wake fly**).

Dorsal fin The fin on the back of a fish, sometimes divided into two or three partly or entirely separate sections.

Drainage A drainage basin or a drainage system; the process of draining.

Drainage basin The catchment area of a river system (*see also* **Basin**).

Drainage system A river and its tributaries.

E

Eddy A patch of water that is less disturbed than the surrounding water, found for instance on the edge of a current or where two streams converge (*see also* **Pool, Riffle, Run, Scour, Slack**).

Electrofishing Passing an electric current through the water to stun the fish, so that they can be collected unharmed for tagging or scientific examination or for relocation to another water.

Esophagus The gullet of a fish.

Euryhaline fish Fish, such as most species of salmon and trout, that can live in both freshwater and saltwater.

F

Fighting chair A swivel chair bolted to the deck of a boat, from which a big-game angler can fight marlin and other large, powerful fish that can take a long time to subdue. The angler is strapped in by a harness, and either the harness or the chair is equipped with a butt pad or rod socket (*see also* **Butt pad**).

Filter feeder A fish that feeds by filtering plankton from the water.

Fingerling A small, immature fish, such as a juvenile trout.

Fish ladder A series of interconnected pools created up the side of a river obstruction, such as a dam, to allow salmon and other fish to pass upstream.

Foul-hook To hook a fish anywhere but in the mouth.

Fresh-run fish A migratory fish, such as a salmon, that has just left the sea and is traveling up a river to spawn.

Freshwater The water of most rivers and stillwaters, containing little or no dissolved salts (*see also* **pH, Salinity**).

Fry Very young fish, especially those that have only recently hatched.

G

Gall bladder A small pouch, on or near the liver of a fish, which stores bile. Bile is a fluid produced by the liver, and aids the absorption of food by the gut.

Gamefish Any fish valued for its sporting qualities (*see also* **Coarse fish, Panfish**).

Gill arch The structure behind the gill covers of a bony fish (or within the gill slits of a cartilaginous fish) that supports the gill filaments and gill rakers.

Gill filaments The parts of a fish's gills that absorb oxygen from the water.

Gill rakers Toothlike projections on the gill arches. They can be used to trap food items, such as plankton, carried in the water flowing through the gills.

Gonads The reproductive organs that are responsible for the production of sperm or eggs (*see also* **Testes, Ovaries**).

Grain A unit of weight, used for instance in

the classification of fly lines. 1 gram = 15.4 grains, 1 oz = 437.6 grains.

Greenheart A tropical American tree, *Ocotea rodiae*; its wood was once used for making fishing rods.

Grilse A young Atlantic salmon making its first spawning run, usually after one and a half to two years in the sea (*see also* **Alevin, Kelt, Parr, Smolt**).

H

Handline A simple tackle rig often used by youngsters fishing from piers and harbor walls. It consists of a sinker and a hook attached to a line that is wound on a wooden or plastic frame.

Hatch The simultaneous surfacing of large numbers of insect nymphs of the same species. At the surface, the adult insects (or duns) emerge from the nymphal cases and usually rest for a while before flying off (*see also* **Rise**).

I

Ice fishing A specialized form of angling, developed in North America, for fishing through holes cut in the ice of frozen-over waters. The species sought include crappies, walleye, northern pike, pickerel, and perch, and the principal techniques are jigging and tilt (or tip-up) fishing. Jigging involves working a natural bait with a short stick, which has a specially shaped handle around which the line is wound. In tilt fishing, the bait is fished static from a rig incorporating an arm or flag that tilts up to signal a bite.

Ichthyology The scientific study of fish and their habits.

IGFA The International Game Fish Association, based in Fort Lauderdale, Florida. It maintains lists of record fish and also sets technical standards for fishing tackle.

Introperculum In bony fish, the front lower bone of the gill cover (*see also* **Operculum, Preoperculum, Suboperculum**).

Invertebrate A creature that has no backbone, for instance an insect or a worm (*see also* **Vertebrate**).

J

Jig A small artificial lure with a metal head, often dressed with feathers.

Jigging Fishing by jerking a jig or other bait up and down in the water; an ice-fishing technique (*see also* **Ice fishing**).

K

Keeper ring A small ring just above the handle of a fishing rod, to which the lure or hook can be attached when not in use.

Kelt A salmon or trout that has spawned (*see also* **Alevin, Grilse, Parr, Smolt**).

Krill Tiny, shrimplike crustaceans, of the family Euphausiidae, that form an essential part of the marine food chain.

L

Lacustrine A term that describes anything of, relating to, or living in lakes.

Ladder See **Fish ladder**
Left bank See **Banks**

Lie A quiet or sheltered spot in the water where a fish can rest, hide from predators, or wait for food to come by.

Limnology The scientific study of lakes and ponds and the plant and animal organisms that live in them.

Livebait Any natural bait, such as a worm, maggot, or small fish, that is used live (*see also* **Deadbait**).

Low-water fly A sparsely dressed fly on a small hook, used mostly for salmon fishing in shallow water.

M

Mark An area of the sea that offers good fishing, usually one that can be located by taking the bearings of shore features.

Marrow spoon A long, slender spoon that can be passed down the gullet of a dead fish to remove its stomach contents. It is used mainly by trout anglers to find out what the fish are actually feeding on at a given time.

Maxillary The rear bone of the upper jaw of a fish (*see also* **Articular, Dentary, Premaxillary, Quadrate**).

Milt The semen of a male fish; a term for the semen-filled testes and sperm ducts of a male fish, also known as soft roe (*see also* **Ova, Roe, Testes**).

N

Neap tides The tides that occur midway between spring tides. They have smaller rises and falls than those at other times of the month (*see also* **Spring tides**).

Nictitating membrane A thin membrane that can be drawn across the eyeball to protect and clean it. Found on many fish species, including some sharks.

O

Operculum In bony fish, the uppermost and largest of the gill cover bones (*see also* **Introperculum, Preoperculum, Suboperculum**).

Osmosis The process by which a fish takes in or excretes water through its skin in order to maintain the correct balance of salts and fluids within its body tissues.

Otoliths Oval, stonelike structures within the ears of a fish or other vertebrate, which help it to maintain its balance; they are also known as ear stones.

Ova The eggs of a fish or other creature. The mass of eggs within the ovarian membranes of a female fish is termed hard roe (*see also* **Milt, Roe, Ovaries**).

Ovaries The reproductive glands (gonads) of a female fish, which are responsible for the production of eggs (*see also* **Testes**).

Oviducts The ducts between the ovaries and vent in most female fish, along which the ripe eggs pass during spawning.

Oviparous fish Fish that lay eggs from which the young later hatch. All skates, some sharks and rays, and most bony fish are oviparous (*see also* **Ovoviviparous fish, Vivipa.ous fish**).

Ovoviviparous fish Fish whose eggs are fertilized and hatched within the female's body. The eggs are enclosed in separate membranes and the embryos within them receive no nourishment from the mother. Most sharks and rays are ovoviviparous (*see also* **Oviparous fish, Viviparous fish**).

P

Panfish Any small American freshwater food fish, such as a sunfish or perch, that is fished for by anglers but is too small to be considered a true gamefish (*see also* **Coarse fish, Gamefish**).

Parabolic-action rod Another term for a through-action rod.

Parr Young salmon and trout up to two years old, distinguishable from smolts by the dark bars (parr marks) on their sides (*see also* **Alevin, Grilse, Kelt, Smolt**).

Pectoral fins The pair of fins just behind the head of a fish.

Pelagic fish Fish that live at the surface, in the upper waters, of the open ocean (*see also* **Demersal fish**).

Pelvic fins The pair of fins on the lower body of a fish; also called ventral fins.

pH The pH number of a liquid, such as water, indicates its acidity or alkalinity. Pure water has a pH of 7; water with a pH of less than 7 is acidic, and water with a pH of more than 7 is alkaline. Acid rain typically has a pH of less than 5.

Pharyngeal teeth Teeth at the back of the throat, found in many fish species such as the members of the carp family. These teeth crush food as it is swallowed (*see also* **Vomerine teeth**).

Pisciculture The breeding and rearing of fish, for example in hatcheries and fish farms.

Pool A relatively wide, rounded area of a river, usually found just downstream of fast, narrow run (*see also* **Eddy, Riffle, Run, Scour, Slack**).

Potamodromous fish Fish that migrate regularly within large freshwater systems (*see also* **Amphidromous fish, Anadromous fish, Catadromous fish**).

Predatory fish Any fish that prey on other living creatures, particularly other fish.

Premaxillary The front bone of the upper jaw of a fish (*see also* **Articular, Dentary, Maxillary, Quadrate**).

Preoperculum In bony fish, the bone at the rear of the cheek, just in front of the gill cover (*see also* **Introperculum, Operculum, Suboperculum**).

Pyloric caeca Fleshy, fingerlike tubes at the junction between the stomach and intestine of a fish. They produce enzymes that play a part in the digestive process.

Q

Quadrate The bone that joins the upper jaw of a fish to its skull (*see also* **Articular, Dentary, Maxillary, Premaxillary**).

R

Rays The soft or spiny supporting elements of fish fins.

Redd A hollow scooped in the sand or gravel of a riverbed by breeding trout or salmon as a spawning area.

Reversed-taper handle A rod handle that tapers toward the butt end.

Riffle A small rapid in a river or stream (see also **Eddy, Pool, Run, Scour, Slack**).

Right bank See **Banks**

Riparian A term that describes anything of, inhabiting, or situated on a riverbank; often used in connection with ownership and fishing rights.

Rip-rap Broken rock, deposited loosely on a riverbed or on the banks to help prevent erosion. It is also used to form breakwaters and embankments.

Rise The action of a fish coming to the surface to take an insect; the taking to the air of a large hatch of mayflies or other insects on which trout feed (see also **Hatch**).

Rod socket See **Butt pad**

Roe A collective term for fish milt and ova (see also **Milt, Ova**).

Run A fast-flowing stretch of river; the movement of fish inshore or upstream for spawning; the flight of a hooked fish trying to escape; a small stream or brook. (See also **Eddy, Pool, Riffle, Scour, Slack**.)

S

Salinity The level of dissolved salts in the water. Freshwater normally contains less than 0.2% salts, brackish water contains up to 3% salts, and saltwater (such as seawater) more than 3%. Normal seawater contains 3.433% salts – 2.3% sodium chloride (common salt), 0.5% magnesium chloride, 0.4% sodium sulphate, 0.1% calcium chloride, 0.07% potassium chloride, and 0.063% other salts.

Saltwater Water containing a high level of dissolved salts (see also **Salinity**).

Scour Erosion caused by flowing water; a shallow, fast-flowing, gravel-bottomed stretch of river (see also **Eddy, Pool, Riffle, Run, Slack**).

Sea anchor A cone-shaped bag, usually made of canvas, which can be trailed behind a drifting boat to slow it.

Seminal vesicle A small gland that adds nutrient fluid to the milt of a male fish during spawning (see also **Milt**).

Sink-and-draw A method of fishing in which the lure, fly, or bait is made to rise and fall alternately during the retrieve by raising and lowering the rod tip.

Sink-tip A floating fly line with a sinking tip, used to fish flies just below the surface.

Slack Tidal water where there is little surface movement during the interval between the ebbing and flowing tides; a stretch of river with very little current, for instance above a dam (see also **Eddy, Pool, Riffle, Run, Scour**).

Slip A narrow strip of feather. Slips are widely used in fly tying.

Smolt A young salmon or sea trout, silver in color, on its first journey to the sea (see also **Alevin, Grilse, Kelt, Parr**).

Spring tides The tides that occur around the time of full and new moons. They have larger rises and falls than those at other times of the month (see also **Neap tides**).

Strike To tighten the line to set the hook when a fish bites, usually by raising the rod tip or lifting the rod.

Suboperculum In bony fish, the rear lower bone of the gill cover (see also **Interperculum, Operculum, Preoperculum**).

Supracleithrum A bone at the upper rear of the skull of a fish. It is one of the bones that support the pectoral fin (see also **Cleithrum, Pectoral fin**).

Surface film The apparent elastic-like film on the surface of water, which is created by surface tension.

Surface tension The natural tendency of the surface of water (and other liquids) to behave like an elastic sheet. It is caused by forces acting between the water molecules: the molecules at the surface are much more strongly attracted to each other, and to the molecules below them, than they are to the molecules of air above them.

Swim The stretch of a river, or the part of a pond or lake, that is being fished in at a particular time.

T

Take The action of a fish in picking up or grabbing a bait or lure.

Taper The narrowing in diameter, from butt to tip, of a rod, and the narrowing of the end section of a fly line. The rate of taper determines the action of the rod or line.

Terminal tackle The tackle, including the hook or lure, attached to the end of the reel line (main line).

Testes (singular: testis) The reproductive glands (gonads) of a male fish, which are responsible for the production of sperm (see also **Ovaries**).

Tilt fishing A technique used in ice fishing; it is also known as tip-up fishing (see also **Ice fishing**).

Tippet The thin end section of a fly leader, to which the fly is tied.

Tube fly An artificial fly consisting of a metal or plastic tube, dressed with feathers, hair, or other materials and threaded onto the line. The hook, usually a treble, is then attached to the end of the line.

V

Vas deferens The duct that carries sperm from the testis of a spawning male fish (see also **Milt, Testes**).

Vent The anus of a fish. It is also the orifice through which a spawning female fish lays her eggs (or, in the case of a viviparous fish, gives birth) and through which a male fish discharges his milt during spawning (see also **Viviparous fish, Milt**).

Vertebra An individual segment of the backbone of a fish.

Vertebrate A creature that has a backbone, for instance a fish or a mammal (see also **Invertebrate**).

Viviparous fish Fish whose ripe eggs are fertilized and hatched within the female's body; they give birth to live young. Unlike those of ovoviviparous fish, the developing embryos receive nourishment from the mother. Some sharks and some bony fish, such as surfperch, are viviparous (see also **Oviparous fish, Ovoviviparous fish**).

Vomerine teeth Teeth on the vomer, a bone at the front of the roof of the mouth of bony fish (see also **Pharyngeal teeth**).

W

Wake fly A dry fly that creates a splashy, fish-attracting wake when pulled across or through the surface of the water (see also **Disturbance pattern**).

Wobbling A freshwater spinning technique using a lure, or a small, dead fish mounted on treble hooks, for bait. The bait is cast a long way out, and retrieved in an erratic fashion by making side-to-side movements of the rod tip and at the same time varying the speed of the retrieve.

Wrist See **Caudal peduncle**

Y

Yolk sac The membrane-covered food pouch found on the belly of a newly hatched fish. It nourishes the growing fish until it is able to feed itself.

INDEX

A

African pompano 51
Alabama spotted bass 10
Albacore 76
Alevin 36
Alewife 79
Allis shad
  description 78
Almaco jack 48
Amberjack
  description 48
  distribution 49
  fishing 49
  schooling 48
  young lesser 49
American
  eel 44
  grayling 41
  plaice 66
  shad 78
Anatomy 8
Arctic
  char 34
  grayling 41
Asp
  description 14
  distribution 15
  fishing 15
  spawning 14
Atlantic
  bonito 79
  cod 57
  hake 57
  halibut 66
  herring 78
  mackerel 74
  salmon 36
  sierra 75
  Spanish mackerel 75
Australian
  bass 28
  blue catfish 46
  bonito 79
  mobula 68
  perch 30
  salmon 72

B

Ballan wrasse 61
Barbel
  barbels of 15
  description 15
  distribution 15
  fishing 15
  food 15
  mouth of 15
  young 15
Barbels (barbules) 15
Barndoor skate 70
Barracuda
  description 46
  distribution 47
  fishing 46
  in shallows 46
  jaws 47
Barramundi
  description 53
  distribution 53
  fishing 52
Barred surfperch 55
Basking shark 82
Bass
  description 28
  distribution 29
  fishing 29

Bass, black *see* **Black bass**
Bat ray 69
Bidyan 30
Big skate 70
Billfish
  description 58
  distribution 59
  fishing 59
  food 58
Black
  bream 30
  bullhead 25
  crappie 13
  drum 72
  grouper 85
  marking 89
  marlin 59
  seabass 84
  seabream 86
  snook 53
Black bass
  description 10
  distribution 11
  dorsal fins 11
  fishing 10
  food 11
Blackfin
  tuna 76
Blacktip shark 81
Blue
  catfish 27
  marlin 59
  runner 48
  shark 83
Blueback herring 79
Bluefin tuna 77
Bluefish
  description 42
  distribution 43
  fishing 42
Bluegill
  description 12
  distribution 13
  fishing 13
Bonefish
  description 42
  distribution 43
  fishing 42
  larva 43
Bonito
  description 78
  distribution 79
  fishing 78
Bonito shark 82
Bony fish 8
Bream
  description 16
  distribution 17
  fishing 17
  food 16
  roach/bream hybrids 16
  young 16
Bronze bream 17
Brook trout 35
Brown
  bullhead 25
  trout 38
Bull
  shark 81
  trout 35
Bullhead
  body shape 24
  description 24
  distribution 25
  fishing 25
  pectoral spines 24

spawning 25
Burbot
  description 56
  distribution 57
  fishing 56

C

Calico surfperch 55
California
  barracuda 47
  corbina 72
  moray 44
  sheephead 60
  skate 70
  yellowtail 49
Cannibal trout 48
Caribbean red snapper 63
Carp
  barbels of 15
  breeding 18
  description 18
  distribution 19
  fishing 18
  food 18
  scales 19
Cartilaginous fish 8
Catfish, freshwater
  barbels of 27
  channel 26
  description 26
  distribution 27
  fishing 26
  food 27
  whiskers of 27
Catfish, sea
  description 46
  distribution 47
  fishing 46
  mouth brooding 46
Cero 74
Chain pickerel 22
Channel catfish 26
Char
  breeding coloration 34
  description 34
  distribution 35
  fishing 34
  hybrids 34
  parr marks 34
Cheetah trout 34
Cherry salmon 36
Chinook salmon 37
Chub
  dace/bleak comparison 20
  description 20
  distribution 21
  fishing 20
  food 20
Chub mackerel 74
Chum salmon 37
Ciguatera 48
Cisco 40
Cobia
  description 52
  distribution 53
  fishing 52
  habitat 52
Cod
  description 57
  distribution 57
  fishing 56
  red 57
Coho salmon 36
Common
  carp 19

pandora 89
skate 71
Crappies
  description 13
  distrbution 13
  fishing 13
Crevalle jack 49
Crucian carp 18
Cuban snapper 63
Cubera snapper 63
Cunner 61
Cutthroat trout 39

D

Dace
  chub/bleak comparison 20
  description 20
  distribution 21
  fishing 20
Danubian
  bream 17
  catfish 26
  roach 21
Devil rays 68
Dolly Varden 35
Dolphinfish
  description 60
  distribution 61
  fishing 60
  head shape 60
Dorado 60
Drum
  description 72
  distribution 73
  fishing 73

E

Eagle rays 69
Eels
  description 44
  distribution 45
  fishing 45
  larvae 44
  marine habitat 45
English sole 66
Estuary perch 31
European
  barracuda 46
  eel 44
  grayling 41
  plaice 66
  porgy 89
  sea bass 29
  whitefish 40

F

Family 7
Fat snook 52
Flat bullhead 25
Flatfish
  description 66
  development 67
  distribution 67
  eggs 66
  fishing 67
  hybrids 66
  larvae 66
Flathead catfish 27
Florida
  largemouth bass 10
  pompano 50
Flounder 66
Freshwater
  catfish 26
  drum 72
  mullet 64

G

Gafftopsail catfish 47
Genus 7
Giant perch 53
Gills 8
Gilt-head
  description 88
  distribution 89
Golden
  barracuda 47
  mullet 65
  perch 31
  tench 14
  trout 39
Goldfish 19
Grass
  carp 19
  pickerel 22
Gray snapper 62
Grayling
  breeding 41
  description 41
  distribution 41
  dorsal fin 41
  dwarfing 41
Great
  barracuda 47
  white shark 83
Greater amberjack 49
Green
  jack 48
  sunfish 12
Grey nurse shark 81
Grilse 37
Grouper
  description 84
  distribution 85
  fishing 85
Grunters
  description 30
  distribution 31
  fishing 30
Guadalupe bass 10
Guaguanche 46
Gudgeon 15
Gulf sierra 75

H

Haddock 57
Hake
  Atlantic 57
  description 57
  fishing 56
  Pacific 57
Halibut 66
Hammerhead shark 83
Hardhead catfish 46
Herring
  Atlantic 78
  blueback 79
  lake 40
  oxeye 43
  river 78
  skipjack 78
Hickory shad 79
Horned pout 25
Horse mackerel 74
Houting 40
Huchen
  range 36
Humpback salmon 36
Hybrids
  Atlantic salmon x sea trout 34
  brook trout x brown trout 34

brook trout x lake trout 34
brook trout x rainbow trout 34
rainbow trout x cutthroat 34
roach x bream 16
starry flounder x English sole 66
Hybrid sole 66

I

Inconnu 40
Irish bream 17

J

Jack
  description 48
  distribution 49
  fishing 49
  schooling 48
Jack (young salmon) 37
Jackmackerel
  description 51
  distribution 51
  fishing 50
Jungle perch 31

K

Kahawai
  description 72
  distribution 73
  fishing 73
Kamloops rainbow 38
Kawakawa 76
Kern river rainbow 38
King
  carp 19
  mackerel 75
  salmon 37
Kokanee 37
Kype 36

L

Ladyfish 43
Lake
  herring 40
  trout 35
  whitefish 41
Landlocked salmon 36
Lane snapper 62
Largemouth bass 10
Largespot mojarra 50
Largetooth sawfish 69
Lateral line 9
Leather carp 19
Leopard shark 80
Lesser amberjack 49
Ling
  description 57
  distribution 57
  fishing 56
Little
  skate 71
  tunny 76
Longbill spearfish 58
Longfin
  bonefish 43
  tuna 76
Longfinned eel 44
Long-nosed skate 71
Longspine porgy 86

M

Mackerel

description 74
distribution 75
eyelids 74
fishing 75
horse 74
Mackerel sharks 81
Macquarie perch 30
Mahi mahi 60
Mako 82
Mangrove
jack 63
snapper 62
Manta 68
Maori wrasse 60
Marlin 59
Marlinsucker 59
Masu salmon 36
Mediterranean barbel 15
Mermaid's purse 68
Mexican barracuda 47
Mirror carp 19
Monterey Spanish mackerel 75
Moray 44
Mountain whitefish 41
Mullet
description 64
distribution 65
fishing 65
Murray cod
description 29
distribution 29
fishing 29
Muskellunge
description 22
distribution 23
fishing 23
food 22
jaws 23
Mutton snapper 62

N
Nase
description 16
distribution 17
fishing 17
Nassau grouper 84
Naturals *see* Flies, natural
Nile perch 53
Northern
pike 22
sennet 46

O
Ouananiche
distribution 37
Oxeye herring (oxeye tarpon) 43

P
Pacific
amberjack 48
barracuda 47
bonito 78
hake 57
halibut 66
porgy 87
salmon 36
sierra 75
Parr 37
Parr marks 34
Pauu'u 49
Perch
description 32
distribution 33
eggs 32
fishing 33
scales 32

Perch, Australian
description 30
distribution 31
fishing 30
spawning estuary perch 31
young golden perch 31
Permit 50
Pickerel
description 22
distribution 23
fishing 23
food 22
jaws 23
Pike
description 23
distribution 23
fishing 23
food 22
jaws 23
Pikeperch 32
Pink salmon 36
Pinkeye 64
Plaice 66
Pollack 56
Pompano
description 50
distribution 51
fishing 50
Pompano dolphin 60
Pope 32
Porbeagle 81
Porgy
description 86
distribution 87
fishing 87
food 86
Powan 40
Pumpkinseed
description 12
distribution 13
fishing 13
gill covers 12

Q
Queensland grouper 85

R
Rainbow trout 38
Rays
description 68
distribution 69
egg cases 68
fishing 69
Red
cod 57
drum 72
grouper 85
mullet 64
porgy 87
salmon 37
seabream 86
snapper 63
Redbreast sunfish 12
Redear sunfish 12
Redeye bass 10
Redfin pickerel 22
Redtail surfperch 55
Remora 59
Requiem sharks 80
River herring 78
Roach
breeding 21
description 21
destribution 21
fishing 20
food 21
roach/bream
hybrids 16

Rock bass 13
Roosterfish
description 51
distribution 51
fishing 50
Roughtail stingray 69
Round
stingray 69
whitefish 41
Rubberlip seaperch 40
Rudd
breeding 21
description 21
fishing 20
food 21
Ruff 72
Ruffe
description 32
distribution 33
fishing 33

S
Sailfish 58
Saithe 56
Salema
description 88
distribution 89
Salmon
alevin 36
breeding coloration 36
description 36
distribution 37
fishing 36
grilse 37
hybrids 34
kype 36
landlocked 36
life cycle 36
migration 36
parr 37
smolt 37
spawning 36
Salmon catfish 46
Salmon shark 81
Sand
seatrout 73
tiger 81
Saucereye porgy 87
Sauger
description 32
distribution 33
fishing 33
Sawfish 69
Scad 74
Scales 9
Schelly 40
Scientific names 7
Scorpion fish
description 88
distribution 89
Scup 86
Sea
catfish 46
trout 38
Sea bream
common two-banded 88, 89
description 86, 88
distribution 87, 89
fishing 87, 89
saddled 88, 89
Sea perch 54
Sebago salmon
distribution 37
Sennets 46
Senorita 60
Shad
description 78
distribution 79

fishing 78
food 78
Shafted bonefish 43
Shark fishing
general 82
Sharks
anatomy 9
blue shark teeth 83
claspers 83
description 80, 82
distribution 81, 83
fishing 82
porbeagle teeth 81
requiem shark tails 83
swimming 9
teeth 81, 83
tope eyes 80
white shark bite 82
Shasta rainbow 38
Sheefish 40
Sheepshead 87
Sheepshead porgy 87
Shiner perch 54
Shortbill spearfish 58
Shortfin
barracuda 47
mako 82
Sierra 75
Silver
bream 17
jack 63
perch 30
salmon 36
seatrout 73
Sixgill shark 82
Skates
description 70
distribution 71
fishing 71
jaws 71
mating 71
undersides of 70
Skimmer bream 16
Skipjack
herring 78
tuna 76
wavyback 76
Smallmouth bass 11
Smalltooth sawfish 69
Smolt 37
Smooth
dogfish 80
hammerhead 83
Snail bullhead 24
Snapper
description 62
distribution 63
fishing 62
juvenile red 63
schooling red 63
Snook
description 52
distribution 53
fishing 52
Sockeye salmon 37
Soiffe 16
Sole 66
Sooty grunter 30
Southern
barbel 15
flounder 66
sennet 46
yellowtail 49
Spanish mackerel 75
Species 7
Spinner shark 81
Splake 34
Spotfin croaker 72
Spotted
bass 10

bullhead 24
ray 68
sea bass 29
seatrout 73
Spurdog 80
Starry flounder 66
Steelhead 38
Stingrays 69
Stone loach 15
Striped
barracuda 47
bass 29
bonito 78
marlin 59
mullet 64
seaperch 55
Sucker (remora) 59
Sunfish
description 12
distribution 13
fishing 13
gill covers 12
Surfperch
description 54
distribution 55
fishing 54
Suwannee bass 10
Swim bladder 8
Swordfish
description 58
distribution 59
fishing 59
food 58

T
Taimen 36
Tandan 26
Tarpon
description 42
distribution 43
fighting ability 42
fishing 42
Tarpon snook 53
Tautog 61
Tench
barbels of 15
description 14
distribution 15
fishing 15
food 14
sex of 14
Tenpounder 43
Thick-lipped grey mullet 65
Thin-lipped grey mullet 65
Thornback ray 68
Threadfish 51
Thresher shark 82
Tiger
shark 83
trout 34
Tinplate bream 16
Tope 80
Toxostome 16
Trevally 49
Trout
cannibal 38
description 34, 38
distribution 35, 39
fishing 34, 38
hybrids 34
Tule perch 54
Tuna
description 76
distribution 77
fishing 77
finlets 77
Tunny 76
Turbot 67
Twaite shad 78

U
Ulua 49
V
Vendace 40
Vimba
description 16
distribution 17
fishing 17
Volga zander 33
W
Wahoo
description 77
distribution 77
finlets 77
fishing 77
jaws 77
Walleye
description 32
distribution 33
fishing 33
Walleye surfperch 54
Warsaw grouper 85
Wavyback skipjack 76
Weakfish 73
Wels 26
Whale shark 82
White
bass 28
catfish 26
crappie 13
croaker 73
mullet 65
perch 28
seabass 72
shark 83
whitebone porgy 87
Whitefish
description 40
distribution 41
fishing 41
Whiteye bream 17
Wichita spotted bass 10
Wild carp 18
Winter
flounder 67
skate 71
Wrasse
description 60
distribution 61
fishing 60
mouth of 61

Y
Yellow
bass 28
bullhead 24
Yellowfin
croaker 72
grouper 84
Yellowstone cutthroat 39
Yellowtail 49

Z
Zährte 16
Zander
description 32
distribution 33
fishing 33
spawning 33

INDEX OF SCIENTIFIC NAMES

A

Abramis
  brama 17
  sapa 17
Acanthocybium
  solanderi 77
Albula
  nemoptera 43
  vulpes 42
Albulidae 42
Alburnus
  alburnus 20
Alectis ciliaris 51
Alopias vulpinus 82
Alosa
  aestivalis 79
  alosa 68
  chrysochloris 78
  fallax 78
  mediocris 79
  pseudoharengus 79
  sapidissima 78
Ambloplites
  rupestris 13
Ameiurus
  brunneus 24
  catus 26
  melas 25
  natalis 24
  nebulosus 25
  platycephalus 25
  serracanthus 24
Amphistichus
  argenteus 55
  koelzi 55
  rhodoterus 55
Anguilla
  anguilla 44
  reinhardtii 44
  rostrata 44
Anguillidae 44
Aplodinotus
  grunniens 72
Archosargus
  probatocephalus 87
Ariidae 46
Arius
  felis 46
  graeffi 46
Arripidae 72
Arripis georgianus 72
  trutta 72
Aspius aspius 15
Atractoscion
  nobilis 72

B

Bargre marinus 47
Barbus
  barbus 15
  meridionalis 15
Bidyanus bidyanus 30

Blicca bjoerkna 16
Bothidae 66

C

Calamus
  arctifrons 87
  bajonado 87
  brachysomus 87
  calamus 87
  leucosteus 87
  penna 87
Carangidae 48, 50
Caranx
  caballus 48
  caninus 48
  crysos 48
  georgianus 49
  hippos 49
  ignobilis 49
  stellatus 49
Carassius
  auratus 19
  carassius 18
Carcharhinidae 80
Carcharhinus
  brevipinna 81
  leucas 81
  limbatus 81
Carcharodon
  carcharias 83
Centrarchidae 10, 12
Centropomidae 52
Centropomus
  nigrescens 53
  parallelus 52
  pectinatus 52
  undecimalis 53
Centropristis
  striata 84
Cetorhinus
  maximus 82
Cheilinus
  undulatus 60
Chelon labrosus 65
Chondrichthyes 9
Chondrostoma
  nasus 16
  toxostoma 16
Clupea harengus 78
Clupeidae 78
Conger conger 45
Congridae 44
Coregonus
  albula 40
  artedi 40
  clupeaformis 41
  pallasi 40
Coryphaena
  equisetus 60
  hippurus 60
Coryphaenidae 60
Ctenopharyngodon
  idella 19
Cymatogaster

aggregata 55
Cynoscion
  arenarius 73
  nebulosus 73
  nothus 73
  regalis 73
Cyprinidae 14, 16, 18, 20
Cyprinus carpio 18, 19

D

Dasyatidae 68
Dasyatis
  centroura 69
Dicentrarchus
  labrax 29
  punctatus 29
Diplodus vulgaris 88, 89

E

Elopidae 42
Elops saurus 43
Embiotoca lateralis 55
Embiotocidae 54
Epinephelus
  itajara 85
  morio 85
  nigritus 85
  striatus 84
Esocidae 22
Esox
  americanus americanus 22
  americanus vermiculatus 22
  lucius 23
  masquinongy 22
  niger 22
Euthynnus
  affinis 76
  alletteratus 76
  pelamis 76
  lineatus 76

G

Gadidae 56
Gadus morhua 57
Galeocerdo cuvieri 83
Galeorhinus galeus 80
Genyonemus
  lineatus 73
Gymnocephalus
  cernuus 32
Gymnothorax
  mordax 44

H

Hephaestus
  fuliginosus 30
Hexanchus
  griseus 83
Hippoglossoides
  platessoides 66
Hippoglossus
  hippoglossus 66

stenolepis 67
Hucho
  hucho 36
  taimen 36
Hyperprosopon
  argenteum 54
Hysterocarpus
  traski 54

I

Ictaluridae 24, 26
Ictalurus
  furcatus 27
  punctatus 26
Istiophoridae 58
Istiophorus
  platypterus 58
Isurus oxyrinchus 82

K

Kuhlia rupestris 31
Kuhliidae 30

L

Labridae 60
Labrus bergylta 61
Lamna
  ditropis 81
  nasus 80
Lamnidae 81
Lates
  calcarifer 53
  niloticus 53
Lepomis 12
  auritis 12
  cyanellus 12
  gibbosus 12
  machrochirus 12
  microlophus 12
Leuciscus
  cephalus 20
  leuciscus 20
Liza
  aurata 65
  ramada 65
Lota lota 56
Lutjanidae 62
Lutjanus
  analis 62
  argentimaculatus 63
  campechanus 63
  cyanopterus 63
  griseus 62
  purpureus 63
  synagris 62

M

Macquaria
  ambigua 31
  austraslica 30
  colonorum 31
  novemaculeata 28
Makaira
  indicus 59
  nigricans 59
  nugricans 59
Manta birostris 68
Megalops

atlanticus 42
cyprinoides 43
Melanogrammus
  aeglefinus 57
Menticirrhus
  undulatus 72
Merluccius
  merluccius 57
  productus 57
Micropterus
  coosae 10
  dolomieui 11
  notius 10
  punctulatus 10
  punctulatus henshalli 10
  punctulatus wichitae 10
  salmoides 11
  salmoides floridanus 10
  treculi 10
Mobula diabola 68
Mobulidae 68
Molva molva 57
Morone
  americana 28
  chrysops 28
  mississippiensis 28
  saxatilis 29
Moronidae 28
Mugil
  cephalus 64
  curema 64
Mugilidae 64
Mullidae 64
Mullus
  surmuletus 64
Muraena helena 44
Muraenidae 344
Mycteroperca
  bonaci 85
  venenosa 84
Myliobatidae 68
Myliobatis
  californica 69
Myxus petardi 64

N

Nematistiidae 50
Nematistius
  pectoralis 51

O

Oblada melanura 88, 89
Odontaspis
  arenarius 81
  taurus 81
Onocorhynchus 34
  aguabonita 39
  clarki 39
  clarki lewisi 39
  gorbuscha 36
  keta 37
  kisutch 36
  masou 36

mykiss 39
nerka 39
tshawytscha 37
Osteichthyes 8
Oxyjulis
  californica 60

P

Pagellus
  bogaraveo 86
  erythrinus 88, 89
Pagrus
  nasutus 86
  pagrus 87
  sparus 89
Paralichthys
  dentatus 66
  lethostigma 66
Parophrys
  vetulus 66
Perca
  flavescens 33
  fluviatilis 33
Percichthyidae 28, 30
Percidae 32
Petrus rupuestris 86
Platichthys
  stellatus 66
Pleuronectes
  platessa 66
Pleuronectidae 66
Plotosidae 26
Pogonias cromis 73
Pollachius
  pollachius 56
  virens 56
Pomatomidae 42
Pomatomus
  saltatrix 42
Pomoxis
  annularis 13
  nigromaculatus 13
Prionace glauca 83
Pristidae 68
Pristis
  pectinata 69
  pristis 69
Promicrops
  lanceolatus 85
Prosopium
  cylindraceum 41
  williamsoni 41
Pseudopleuronectes
  americanus 67
Pylodictis olivaris 27

R

Rachycentridae 52
Rachycentron
  canadum 52
Raja
  alba 71
  batis 71

binoculata 70
clavata 68
eglanteria 70
erinacea 71
inornata 70
laevis 70
montagui 68
ocellata 71
oxyrinchus 71
Rajidae 68, 70
Rajiformes 68, 70
Rhacochilus
  toxotes 54
Rhincodon typus 82
Roncador
  stearnsii 72
Rutilis
  pigus pigus 21
  pigus virgo 21
  rutilus 21

S

Salmo 7, 34
  salar 36
  trutta 7, 38
Salmonidae 7, 34, 36, 38, 40
Salvelinus
  alpinus 34
  confluentus 35
  fontinalis 35
  malma 35
  namaycush 35
Sarda
  australis 79
  chiliensis 79
  chiliensis chiliensis 78
  chiliensis lineolata 78
  orientalis 78
Sarpa salpa 88, 89
Scardinius
  erythrophthalmus 21
Sciaenidae 82
Sciaenops
  ocellatus 82
Scomber
  japonicus 75
  scombrus 74
Scomberomorus
  brasiliensis 75
  cavalla 75
  commerson 75
  concolor 75
  guttatus 75
  maculatus 74
  regalis 75
  sierra 75
Scombridae 74, 76
Scophthalmus
  maximus 67
Scorpaena
  porcus 88, 89
  scarfa 88, 89
Scorpaenidae 88,

89
Selachii 80, 82
Semicossyphus
  pulcher 60
Seriola
  colburni 48
  dumerili 49
  fasciata 49
  grandis 49
  lalandi 49
  lalandi dorsalis
    49
  rivoliana 48
Serranidae 84

Siluridae 26
Siluris glanis 26
Soleidae 66
Sparidae 86, 88
Sparus
  aurata 86, 88
  pagrus 88, 89
Sphyraena
  argentea 46
  barracuda 46
  borealis 46
  ensis 47
  guachancho 46
  novae-

hollandiae 47
obtutasta 47
picudilla 46
sphyraena 46
Sphyraenidae 46
Sphyrna zygaena
  83
Spondyliosoma
  cantharus 86
Squalus acanthias
  80
Stenodus
  leucichthys 40
Stenotomus

caprinus 86
chrysops 86
Stizostedion
  canadense 32
  lucioperca 33
  vitreum 32
  volgensis 33

T

Tandanus
  tandanus 26
Tautoga onitis 61
Tautogolabrus
  adspersus 61

Teraponidae 30
Tetrapturus
  angustirotris
    58
  audax 58
  belone 58
  pfluegeri 58
Thunnus
  alalunga 77
  atlanticus 76
  thynnus 77
Thymallidae 40
Thymallus
  arcticus 41

thymallus 41
Tinca tinca 14
Trachinotus
  botla 50
  carolinus 50
  falcatus 50
Trachurus
  symmetricus 51
  trachurus 74
Triakis
  semifasciata 80

U

Umbrina

roncador 72
Urolophus halleri
  69

V

vimba vimba 16

X

Xiphias gladius 58
Xiphiidae 58

ACKNOWLEDGMENTS

This book was the work of a dedicated team of authors, photographers, and illustrators, plus a huge network of specialists and suppliers, to whom we would like to express our gratitude.

First, thanks to Martin at Photo Summit, whose coffee and excellent prints helped to get the book started; to John Wilson for his time, hospitality, and advice; to Mike Millman for his help and his willingness to try the impossible at short notice; to Ron Worsfold for the loan of his pole tigs; and to the late and much-missed Trevor Housby for his advice and encouragement.

Of all our suppliers, special mention must by made of Don Neish and Peter Morley at Don's of Edmonton, for supplying tackle at ludicrously short notice. Other individuals and companies whose contrbutions were especially valuable were Simon Bond (Shimano); Alan Bramley and Fiona Humus (Partidge of Reddtich); Bob Brownsdon (Shakespeare); Peter Drennan and daughter Sally (Drennan International); Sue and Chris Harris (Harris Angling Company); Chris Leibbrandt (Rylobi Masterlind); David McGinlay (Daiwa); and John Rawle (Cox & Rawle).

We would also like to thank Richard Banbury (Orvis); Breakaway Tackle; Browning; Paul Burgess (Airflo); Jeremy Buxton (Asset Optics); Pat Byrne (D.A.M.); Alan Caulfield (Penn); Darren Cox (DCD); Roy Eskins (HUFFishing); Brendan Fitzgerald (House of Hardy); Michael McManus (Carroll McManus); Nick Page (Nican Enterprises); Gaeme Pullen (Blue Water Tackle); Andrew Rade (Keenets); Nicholas Stafford-Deitsch (Edington Sporting Co.); Mike Stratton (Thomas Turner & Sons); B.W. Wright (Nomad); Val and Chris (Vanguard

Tackle, Boston); Bruce Vaughan and Dennis Moss (Wychwood Tackle); Clive Young (Young's of Harrow); and Rick Young (Leeda).

Finally, special thanks to Barbara, Hilary, and Jane for their support in difficult times; to the unflappable Janet at Ace; to Steve, Andy, Tim, Nick, Sara, and Gary at the studio; to Krystyna and Derek at Dorling Kindersley for their patience; and to Peter Kindersley, whose confidence allowed it to happen.

CREDITS

Illustrators
Colin Newman
pages 8–87

Photographers
6 Oxford Scientific Films / Richard Davis
7 Oxford Scientific Films / Rudolf Ingo Reipl

Manufacturers and Suppliers
Airflo, Fly Fishing technology Ltd., Powys;
Asset Optics, Oxfordshire;
Blue Water Tackle, Hampshire;
Breakaway Tackle, Suffolk;
Browning, Bedfordshire;
Carroll McManus Ltd., East Sussex;
Cox & Rawle, Essex;
Daiwa Sports Ltd., Strathclyde;
D.A.M. (UK) Ltd., Worcestershire;
DCD, Warwickshire;
Don's of Edmonton, London;
Drennan International Ltd., Oxford;
Edington Sporting Co., Wiltshire;
Harris Angling Company, Norfolk;
House of Hardy, London;
HUFFishing, Bedfordshire;
Keenets (UK) Ltd., Wiltshire;
Leeda Group, Worcestershire;
Nican Enterprises, Hampshire;

Nomad UK, Lancashire;
Orvis, Hampshire;
Partridge of Redditch, Worcestershire;
Penn UK, Strathclyde;
Ryobi Masterlind Ltd., Gloucestershire;
Shakespeare Company (UK) Ltd., Worcestershire;
Shimano Europe, Swansea;
Thomas Turner & Sons, Berkshire;
Vanguard Tackle, Lincolnshire;
Wychwood Tackle, Oxfordshire;
Youngs of Harrow, Middlesex.